THE HOLOCAUST LESSONS ON COMPASSIONATE PARENTING AND CHILD CORPORAL PUNISHMENT

David A Cooperson, MSW, MA, LCSW

ISBN: 1493789430
ISBN 13: 9781493789436
Library of Congress Control Number: 2014900947
CreateSpace Independent Publishing Platform
North Charleston, South Carolina

"Children are not for hitting."
—Dr. Haim Ginott

"First and foremost we do not believe in spanking because it hasn't been shown to be effective in changing behavior, because it's allowing parents to vent their own stress, and because it teaches your child to be more aggressive to others (mirror neurons, people)! That's not to mention the fact that spanking is associated in some research with lower IQs in people." ([Mirror neurons will be discussed later in the book.)]
—Dr. Mehmet Oz, MD, and Michael F. Roizen, MD

ACKNOWLEDGEMENTS

When I retired, I reignited my relationship with Judaism, and I thank the writers, rescuers, and researchers of the Holocaust for adding a missing piece to my studies of child rearing and the Jewish perspective on child corporal punishment. I thank the "invisible heroes", social workers who day to day protect children from abuse under conditions that sometimes are reminiscent of a war zone.

My experiences at the Philadelphia Department of Human Services forged my views on children's lack of legal protection from physical punishment. I thank the many advocates opposed to corporal punishment of children under immense odds. I have listed some of these warriors at the end of the book. They choose not to be bystanders.

First, I thank my son, Sol, who recently received his PhD in communications disorders and has been extremely supportive of my work. My wife, Nancy, is a family physician who believes in the message of this book from a medical perspective and has been a rock. My first wife, Vivian, who died of cancer after nearly twenty-five years of marriage, showed me that keeping up with the latest science, teaching skills, and maintaining discipline in the classroom with children enables an educator to avoid meting out physical punishment and still keep order, even in some challenging Philadelphia schools. I thank my brother, Dan who was my inspiration as he fought through many childhood obstacles and worked tirelessly in the child protective field as a social worker. He turned his experiences into fuel for helping others. I thank my parents, who, in spite of their troubled childhoods, spent a lifetime of learning, opening their minds, and trying to repair relationships with their children. The letters my mother wrote at age ninety-two demonstrated her painstaking learning about the futility of child corporal punishment.

TABLE OF CONTENTS

This chapter discusses the fact that "never again" should mean "never again." There were many lessons on human relations that were researched as a result of the Holocaust. A famous collection of studies was in *The Authoritarian Personality* by Adorno, Frenkel-Brunswick, Levinson, and Sanford. They warned about harsh childhood conditions as a breeding ground for violence. Other studies, such as those by Samuel P. Oliner and his wife, Pearl, focused on raising children without physical punishment. A scholar and a survivor, Samuel was obsessed with the reasons some non-Jews in the Nazi-occupied countries, about one-half of 1 percent, protected the Jews and rescued them from Nazi persecution at great risk to themselves. He found in an extensive sample of rescuers that a major factor was that they had received negligible physical punishment as children compared to a group that did not attempt to rescue the Jews.

We examine some of the research and theories about teaching Holocaust lessons in light of the child corporal punishment issue. Next we review the New School for Social Research in New York City, which was begun to allow the scholars who were persecuted in countries like Germany to have a research institute where they also teach. They have professors and courses that are relevant to the issue at hand. The real-life experiences of the Nazi era cannot help but resonate in the lessons at this dynamic school.

Pro-spankers of children are not of like mind and have a confusing list of how, when, who, at what age, and under what conditions it is acceptable for parents to spank their children. Rosemond, a prolific writer, dismisses thirty years of research and clinical experience that non-spankers cite as invalid despite the fact that well over 90 percent of the studies demonstrate the danger to children who receive corporal punishment in school and at home. With a wide brush, he dismisses this mountain of research and the techniques learned for nonphysical punishment as psychobabble. But isn't psychobabble in the eye of the beholder?

In about 1850, a young child was being badly beaten and neglected, but there were no laws to protect her. Therefore advocates had to plead with the Society for Protection of Animals to expand its reach to a novel concept: protecting this child and the many who, up to this point, were ignored by the law.

My mother and father had painful childhoods and tried to be loving parents, but they had no role models. In addition, society "gave permission" for a degree of maltreatment with its history of treating children as property who could be physically punished at a parent's whim with precious few regulations or laws to protect them. Today, children's rights are still on our civil rights "shopping list." When you learn of my family tree, which was riddled with physical punishment mixed with moments of tenderness and inconsistency, you will see what led me to advocate for the issue of legally protecting children from physical punishment, a position that is not popular and, to a great degree, invisible.

All fifty states have sanctimoniously set up laws to stop the bullying of children, but the blinders are on when it comes to school corporal punishment in over a third of our states. What's with that as Seinfeld would say!

This chapter argues that the thirty years of scientific studies plus the advances of neuroscience and physiology in recording the effects of maltreatment of children are in fact like an iceberg that is not seen well by American politicians and the public. Social policy is in the ice age as well, frozen in time while advancing one small thaw at a time.

Yes, there is a sports hero, later a state representative, who has taken up the cause of nonphysical punishment of children, but he is in the minority, and his effect is minimized by his own political party. That is just the beginning.

This chapter provides the context leading to the final arguments in this book concerning stopping physical punishment of children.

This chapter explores the importance of keeping an open mind and examines the long-term trends toward treating children more humanely, as some of our punishment tactics are a continuation on a lesser scale of the history of children as property. Examining the relationship between the nature and nurture principles and the rise of epigenetics is a context that may make more sense of the historic horrors of childhood and the progress that is gradually happening. Lastly, Holocaust research is a treasure that should not be ignored for the well-being of our children and for other lessons about having a less violent world.

CHAPTER 1

THE HOLOCAUST AND THE SAFETY OF TODAY'S CHILDREN

Yes, there is hope. The pro-spanking advocates of today are a tamer lot than the old-time pro-spanking supporters. There has been excruciatingly slow progress on ending school corporal punishment and even progress to a much lesser extent in easing home corporal punishment. For the safety of children, this needs to continue at a more rapid rate.

Advocates for spanking based on religious beliefs, such as James Dobson and John Rosemond, whose positions will be examined later, would be considered weak-kneed by the past fundamental religious groups of the Puritan vintage. Religious denominations such as Methodism and Judaism have shown growth in protecting children. The Methodist church has, over the past decades, changed its tenets and now has official policies opposing corporal punishment of children based on understanding years of research, and the belief that Jesus would in fact not wish children to have their inborn sins beaten out of them. Modern-day Methodists differ from their founder, John Wesley, who was vehement in his call for painful, physical punishment as a duty, even with newborn babies, to correct that original sin predilection. Since 2000, Israel has rendered corporal punishment of children unlawful in both schools and homes, despite a history in which corporal punishment was advocated for children by many religious interpretations and scholars.

I must admit that the journey to opposing corporal punishment of children only came to me after years of working with troubled families and maltreated children. This work experience, combined with intense study of the thirty years of research on the topic, a reassessment of my parents' life experiences, and the years of therapy I have received since the age of thirteen years have molded the evolution of my position.

I also know how difficult it is to change traditions and long-held family practices. At first I was angry and impatient that the United States, with its emphasis on individual rights, has to this day short-changed children's safety. Now I am still impatient but less angry as I realize how the human factor must be understood.

One of the principal forces in advocating physical punishment of children is religion. *Breaking Their Will: Shedding Light on Religious Child Maltreatment*, Janet Heimlich's well-researched book on both the history and current state of child maltreatment, cites a mountain of examples of religious denominations and parents maltreating children in the name of religion. The examples she cites are not just in the past but current.[1] She discusses how Phillip Greven, author of *Spare the Child: The Religious Roots of Punishment and the Psychological Impact of Physical Abuse*, states that "breaking the will of children, even babies" is still practiced by many conservative

Christians,[2] and recent pro-spanking authors have advocated for this treatment of children.

The extreme Orthodox branch of Judaism, by tradition, adore and nurture their children. However at times because outside communities have persecuted them for centuries have concern about the state protecting their children. Out of a desire to protect the children may provide safe havens for child abusers in their communities, as they encourage keeping most problems within the community. They may shun informants who alert the outside secular world. But there is another powerful trend in Judaism to question the practices of the past, with Israel itself leading the way as an example of protecting children from corporal punishment by adults. Since, perhaps, the most powerful "justification" for physical punishment of children is religion, I will argue for another religious perspective on this issue: what can we learn from the Holocaust?

Marcus Fabius Quintillianus, known as Quintillian, AD 40–118, was tired of telling people that children should not receive physical punishment. He felt that enough information was available then to demonstrate the danger and barbaric nature of physical punishment of children: "It is a disgraceful form of punishment...moreover when children are beaten, pain or fear frequently have the result of which it is not pleasant to speak and likely subsequently a source of shame, which unnerves and depresses the mind and leads the child to shun the light of day and loathe the light... I will not linger on the subject. It is more than enough, if I have made my meaning clear."[3]

I feel that over two thousand years later, we have enough scientific studies and new techniques that we should already know how harmful it is to physically punish children. However, we do not. Therefore, I have to spend time on this matter that Quintillian thought they should have known literally ages ago. Quintillian was a Roman scholar, but, at about the same time, a Greek philosopher, Plutarch, said, "Children ought to be led to honorable practices by means of encouraging and reasoning, and most certainly not by blows and ill treatment."[4]

Thirty years of research on the danger of school corporal punishment is denied or shunned by our Congress and politicians in the nineteen American states where it is legal, as well as by too many educators and the public. Furthermore, two recent bills focused on ending legalized corporal punishment (usually paddling) in schools in all states died without leaving the congressional committee for a vote. It is necessary to disseminate the information, as they say, by any means necessary. Book after book and research article after research article are denied, dismissed, or deemed invisible. The Holocaust spawned voluminous research studies, which could be of immeasurable worth to society. One of the lessons concerns corporal punishment of children.

LESSONS ABOUT CORPORAL PUNISHMENT FROM HOLOCAUST RESCUERS AND SURVIVORS

Fast-forward to the present. In 2013, The Holocaust Museum featured the exhibit "Some Were Neighbors: Collaboration and Complicity during the Holocaust." The curator, Susan Bachrach, believed the museum did not sufficiently allow the visitors to feel the conflict of aiding the Jews or being a bystander.[5] They could see governments and military as to blame and distance themselves from thinking, *What would I have done?* Ordinary people were the "instruments" of the atrocities. Through this idea of rescuers who refused to be "instruments" or bystanders, I will demonstrate how physical punishment of children is a factor in whether people stand up for each other when danger is present. Through learned survivors, we will examine how physical punishment of children became such a central part of their theories and research and how dramatically different paths drove this point home.

To this I present the following quote from Dr. Robert Fathman: "Only one country ever reinstated corporal punishment in schools after it was banned. Only one political entity did so—Nazi Germany. It has of course been banned in the present German State."[6] Learning from the past is his message. We will see how adults have failed to learn lessons about Jewish children from the Holocaust and its devastating effect on us all.

Samuel P. Oliner is one of these Holocaust children who barely survived. Out of unimaginable terror, he has crafted a lifetime as a scholarly witness bearer whose lessons painfully spurred stirring research that barely sees the light of day.[7]

Samuel was born in the eastern part of Poland in 1930. It was not enough that his mother died when he was seven, but then his father moved away to have a new life and family. His maternal grandparents raised him. After the Jews were persecuted and mandated to wear yellow stars, he moved back with his dad, stepsiblings, and stepmother. They lived in the Bobowa ghetto, where Jews were terrorized, starved, and beaten. With death and disease rampant, Samuel would risk his life to leave the ghetto and steal food to keep his family alive. In 1942, all residents of this ghetto were murdered. Samuel survived only because his stepmother begged him to leave to the countryside. He learned to feign being a Catholic and lived with a Polish family whose members risked their lives to keep him alive. A million and a half children were killed, but only these Polish rescuers kept him from joining that number.

Samuel was galvanized to find out why fewer than one half of 1 percent non-Jews were rescuers in the Nazi occupied territory. He made it his life's mission to find out why some people, later called the Righteous Christians, risked their lives to save fellow humans who were marked for death.

Samuel painstakingly gained an education, receiving a PhD in sociology from the University of California at Berkeley, one of the most respected universities in the United States. He researched and interviewed rescuers to determine which characteristics made them so different. One of the most significant results he had was that these rescuers, as compared to a control group, had received almost no physical punishment or spanking as children. Their parents took the time to reason with and educate them and to problem solve if they were on the wrong track behaviorally.

> *Parents played a very influential role for both rescuers and non-rescuers, however, significantly more rescuers perceived their parents as benevolent figures, modeling values conducive to forming close, caring attachments to other people who might be different by virtue of status, ethnicity, or religion. When the rescuers were disciplined as children, they had been talked to, and the consequences of their misbehavior had been explained to them, rather than being disciplined physically. Non-rescuers were more likely to have been spanked...[8]*

Sociologist Robert Grille supports Oliner's research and the importance of it not being on the back burner in America and other countries:

There is probably no clearer evidence that childhood shapes society. There is no more compelling and convincing imperative to abandon violent and punitive child rearing methods. The willingness to take altruistic action, even when this poses a risk, and the willingness to defy dishonorable authority, these are sins of emotional maturity—the product of non-violent and respectful child rearing. If more Europeans had been raised this way around the turn of the 20th century, there would not have been a Holocaust.[9]

The Holocaust denier, at least on the surface, is hated in the United States as the cruelest of creatures. However to *deny* or fail to learn the lessons of the Holocaust is a path that has made the United States less of a compassionate country when it comes to the most vulnerable in its midst. The child is the father to the man, and there are volumes to be learned from the horrors of the children of the Holocaust. Perhaps the lessons of the Holocaust are a reason Israel eventually adopted a nationwide policy of outlawing corporal punishment in school and at home. Perhaps that is a reason so many children of Holocaust survivors chose to pursue helping professions, such as psychology, social work, medicine, and nursing, whose professional societies officially and vehemently oppose corporal punishment of little ones, at least in school. As a matter of fact, the American Bar Association opposes it as well.

In a concrete effort to apply his research findings to the realities of the world, Samuel Oliner started an institute at Humboldt State University to study and research prosocial and altruistic behaviors and social policies. This institute is now led by Professor Ronnie Swartz, director of the Altruistic Personality and Prosocial Behavior Institute at Humboldt State University, who stated by return e-mail, "I, *too*, think it is outrageous that school corporal punishment is still allowed in some communities... It's a topic I cover in several courses."

Many research studies, driven by the Holocaust, were in *The Authoritarian Personality* by Adorno, Frenkel-Brunswick, Levinson, and Sanford. In their extensive studies of a large body of interviews, they found that "prejudiced subjects tend to report a relatively harsh and more threatening parenting which was experienced as arbitrary by the child." This supports Oliner's studies and the mountain of research about the harm of corporal punishment.[10]

Eva Fogelman, another Holocaust researcher and survivor, researched and studied the rescuers.[11] She supported Oliner's assertion that being treated with empathy and compassion and a lack of physical punishment as children was a major factor in the motivation and emotional makeup of the Righteous Christians.

It is worth noting that it was not just Christians who rescued children during the Holocaust. For example, Janusz Korczak was a Jewish rescuer of Jewish children, as well as a pediatrician, an educator, the head and founder of orphanages, and a writer of children's books.[12] Because of his stature as a scholar, he was well respected and was offered the opportunity to be considered an Aryan by the Nazis and to let his orphans go alone into concentration camps. He refused and chose to join his orphans to the death camps to provide comfort. He, too, was exterminated. His books are considered of the highest moral fabric. One was *The Child's Right to Respect* (Korczak, 2009), which was based on his lectures. Experts and child advocates expanded these ideas in this documented lecture series. This book presented many rights that children should have, and the right to be free of corporal punishment was one of them. (This was twenty years after my father was an orphan, when he and others were often spanked, beaten, and mistreated). Under the pressure of possible death, Korczak did not waver in his protection of children. Oliner points out that many of the persons who knew Korczak from the orphanage and through other professional contacts chose to become social workers from the stellar role modeling.[13]

Again we see the theme of Holocaust rescuers having been raised with negligible corporal punishment and then protecting children in a heroic manner and vehemently advocating for freedom from physical punishment of any kind. Korczak wrote books, prior to the Holocaust, on understanding child development and recognizing the frustrations to both the child and the caretaker. He recommended that parents take time to know themselves as a prelude and condition of caring for children. If Jews had saints, he surely would be one. But I will say that he was a super-mensch. He was advanced in his study and understanding of child development, which was not studied in earnest until the 1970s. As a child, he played with blocks and made fortresses, where he engaged in imaginary wars to fight for child welfare and rights. In staying with his "childish" games of advocating for children, he was in fact in a war to protect those children, which would ultimately cost him his own life in the concentration camp.. He had fought to change the culture of the orphanages that were notorious for harsh treatment and physical punishment of children. In his era, orphans became known as "citizens." When my father was an orphan twenty years earlier, they were called "inmates" in an official document, and there were countless accounts of brutal treatment and physical beatings of children, but also accounts of caring individuals, causing these confused orphans to never know what to expect. (More will be forthcoming about this era.)

It was not just the orphans who were subjected to beatings. For instance, Irmgard Hunt was a German child who felt the sting of German authoritarianism in her school. She wrote this in a chapter called "Learning to Hate School" (2006). Her teacher Fraulein Stohr frequently used physical punishment on the students for the mildest of offenses, as did most of the other educators. Hunt's own mother, whom Irmgard otherwise adored, was afraid to stand up to this teacher.[14] Other children in her class were also punished, although the school was in a mountainous area that was home to many prominent Nazis, including Albert Speer. His son was one of Hunt's classmates, and the school was strongly programmed to believe in corporal punishment.

In the area of humanity, the Holocaust rescuers chose to risk their well-being to save Jews; they had received gentle, caring, nonphysical correction methods as children, in contrast to the strict, systematic, physically coercive methods of child rearing that was pervasive in the territories Hitler annexed, especially Germany itself. This style was used even with infants and very young children. Dr. Schreber and other German child "experts" inundated the populace with publications that encouraged a tough, unyielding treatment of infants. There are the writings of Morton Schatzman (1974), who studied Shreber and noted his insistence that babies be stopped from crying, which swept well-meaning parents into this control frenzy.[15] Alice Miller also points out that the latest research on the brain development of children cautions against such punitive measures for children.[16] Infants' brains are works in progress and require warm, supportive interactions with their caregivers to properly blossom.

The strict child-rearing style was used by gentiles and Jews alike in pre–World War II Germany, at least according to Susan Kushner Resnick, author of *You Saved Me Too: What a Holocaust Survivor Taught Me about Living, Dying, Fighting, Loving and Swearing in Yiddish* (2013). Resnick learned about life from a ninety-four-year-old Holocaust survivor, Aron, who was alone and whom she befriended in a close relationship for fifteen years. One of the topics Resnik and Aron discussed was corporal punishment of children and how in the 1920s it was rampant in the Jewish community and was learned from former generations.[17] Members of a family from the 1920s were bitter for years after growing up in a home where spanking was a staple, and the children learned to imitate and hit each other. The survivor taught Resnick that patience and understanding were the best ways to raise children. The Holocaust survivor had learned from the Holocaust that how his generation was raised is not the way to go. This meshes with the teachings of Oliner (1988), and Fogelman (1994). Resnick was a young mother at the time she bonded with the survivor and was enriched in raising her children by his experience.

CAUTIONARY LESSONS FROM THE HOLOCAUST: BRUNO BETTELHEIM

Although the survivors of the Holocaust are among the noblest, most caring people that I ever read about or met, even their human weaknesses and conflicts can teach us a lesson on how to live. One survivor, Dr. Bruno Bettelheim (1987), became a world-famous child psychologist who was considered a valued expert on the caring, discipline, and development of children. He was also considered an esteemed expert on autism. He was the head of a prominent school that worked with the most troubled of children.

He also wrote several books that were best sellers, drawing on his experiences in the Holocaust to show the need for love, respect, and gentle discipline of children. He was opposed to any corporal punishment of children, asserting, "Punishment may make us obey orders, but at best it will only teach obedience to authority, not a self-control, which has self-respect."[18] Bettelheim wrote *Surviving and Other Essays*; *Auschwitz*; *A Good Enough Parent: A Book on Child-Rearing, Freud, and Man's Soul*; *The Empty Fortress: Infantile Autism and the Birth of the Self*; *The Children of the Dream*; *The Uses of Enchantment: The Meaning and Importance of Fairy Tales*; *The Informed Heart*; *The Art of the Obvious*; and *Freud's Vienna and Other Essays*, to name some of his works. He was in many ways an icon.

So popular was Bettelheim on TV interview programs that I could not garner a ticket to the June 2, 1972 David Frost show in Manhattan, where he was interviewed. This was surprising, considering that when I was short on money I had often gone to the free Dick Cavett and David Frost television shows and had seen many famous stars in all endeavors. (The only psychologist that I had an opportunity to see in person on one of those shows was Dr. Haim Ginott, who would prove to be the anti-Bettelheim for me, along with Holocaust survivor and survivor researcher Samuel P. Oliner, whom I unfortunately only studied from afar.)

Despite Dr. Bettelheim's renown, he was split at least in two. Although he championed protecting children, he fooled his book readers, the television hosts on whose programs he was often the lead guest, the television audiences that idolized him, and experts in the field of psychiatry and psychology.

The world gasped when he died at his own hand at eighty-six, and his past unraveled at warp speed. Countless students complained that he had beaten them and terrified them to the point that they did not speak up. This is a classic example of how an abusive family works: hiding the truth and keeping secrets. Even one of his students at the University of Chicago, which he had tricked into giving him a professorship, said that while he used the corporal punishment he denied, he was really a loving and skilled therapist and caretaker of children.

It was learned that Bettelheim had faked his world-class university training in psychology, psychiatry, and psychology. He actually had an art history doctorate. Not only was he a dangerous man concerning advice on how to discipline children, but Bettelheim also had a respected theory about autism that was proven to be false. He blamed it all on the "cold," distant mother, and the "refrigerator mom" myth was fostered.

This will prove interesting later in this book, as children and some adults tend to bully children who they perceive as weaker, such as children with autism. They are the ones, along with minority races, to receive a disproportionate amount of physical punishment by teachers in schools in states where it is oh-so-legal.

Similarly, Bettelheim preyed on weaker children who had autism, other disabilities, and emotional problems with physical force that he pretended did not occur. Perhaps this behavior of Bettelheim demonstrates a well-known psychological occurrence: identification with the aggressor. That is, one such as Bettelheim, who was persecuted and punished by the Nazis, may have unwittingly or unconsciously adopted their use of force to control his environment in a way to feel invulnerable.

Bettelheim stated, "Not only is our love for children tinged with annoyance, discouragement, and disappointment, the same is true for the love our children feel for us."[19]

Roberta Carly Redford, in *Crazy: My Seven Years at Bruno Bettelheim's Orthogenic School,*[20] describes how Bettelheim slapped and beat children, and nobody questioned him because he was considered an icon in his field. He had a powerful and intimidating style that even his University of Chicago colleagues and academic leaders admired. This demonstrates how even severe physical maltreatment can be hidden, much as, say, a domineering, abusive father in a family of secrets can go unreported.

IS PHYSICALLY ABUSING OTHERS "NORMAL" HUMAN BEHAVIOR?

The research cited in this chapter makes it clear that historically, people who were willing to protect children from physical abuse were in the minority. And those who were willing to defend children in the Holocaust tended to come from family backgrounds in which corporal punishment was unheard of. Is there something about growing up in an authoritarian regime that makes adults more brutal toward children, though, or is physical abuse of weaker individuals "normal" human behavior?

Stanley Milgram, a Jewish research psychologist at Yale University, was perplexed and tormented by the fact that in Nazi Germany almost everyone followed the authoritarian dictates by assisting or being a bystander as Jews and other minorities were sent to concentration camps to be slaughtered. This intense questioning led to a research study (1974) to investigate what might or might not have been "normal" human behavior under an extreme authoritarian regime.[21] He arranged equipment that appeared to give off electric shocks to people that could be controlled in terms of intensity and duration. Milgram had assistants encourage subjects to keep on increasing the shock level to other participants who were "confederates"; they pretended that as the electric surge grew higher, they were in more pain. To his surprise, almost all of the subjects were convinced by the assistants to continue increasing the shocks even though the recipients feigned pain and agony with each increment. This is one of the most well-known psychological experiments in history.

Milgram also wrote about how small children can be affected by authority issues. If a parent tells a child not to hit another smaller child, there are actually two sets of commands there. The first is a moral injunction not to hurt a more vulnerable human being. The second is an authoritative injunction to obey the command. Just think about what happens when a teacher or parent tells a child not to hit another child and then plies the child with physical punishment.

He was "shocked" to how significant numbers in the study chose to follow authority even when cringing from the effects on others from the jolts they "delivered". Hurting others too often appeared to be a "normal response to the follow the leader scenario.

CHAPTER 2

WHY HASN'T THE UNITED STATES LEARNED FROM THE HOLOCAUST LESSONS?

Many countries in the world have made corporal punishment in school illegal.

A number of countries have also made corporal punishment at home illegal as well. The United States is, to a degree, mired in the past when it comes to this issue. There are more than 100 countries in the world where school corporal punishment is banned and over 31 countries where corporal punishment is banned in all circumstances including the home.

In fact, there are only two countries in the United Nations (out of close to two hundred) that have not ratified the United Nations Bill of Rights for Children that rejected the physical punishment of children. Only Somalia, which is basically lawless, and the United States have not ratified this agreement. President George Bush Sr. was opposed to the measure, as he felt states' rights were more sacred than children's rights.

"For most of our history, Americans have been in denial about child abuse."[22] This quote from Barbara Woodhouse (2008) implies that we are beginning to lift the denial about how children are overlooked when it comes to rights that other adult human beings take for granted. "Childhood is a nightmare from which we are just beginning to wake."[23] This quote from Lloyd DeMausse (1975) also shows that progress is being made in who needs protection, but on a slow learning curve.

Children's rights in the United States received a hit below the belt when, in 1977, the US Supreme Court ruled that a boy who was held down by teachers and hit with a paddle at least twenty times, causing severe bruising and difficulty with movement, did not undergo cruel and unusual punishment. Had this happened to any other citizen who did not happen to be a child, the perpetrators would have been arrested and held accountable by law. But justice is too often blind when it comes to our most vulnerable citizens, the children. The vast majority of court decisions have favored the rights of educators to use corporal punishment on children even when the consequences bordered on dire. In *Hidden in Plain Sight,* Barbara Bennett Woodhouse states that "children are not playing on a level playing field with adults, including the adults they will one day become, when it comes to understanding and doing right."[24]

In *Willful Blindness,* Margaret Heffernan discusses the staggering amount of child abuse and maltreatment that is denied by American families as a type of blindness that we are not willing or able to face head on in our national policies.[25] Hitler 's policies reflect his combative stance that considered children unclean and wild and stained with deep shame. No wonder his society reinstated corporal punishment in schools. Grille points out that Germans were particularly strict on children. This is reflected in children's manuals in Germany at that time. Germans were behind Western society on women's rights and humane childcare, but since the horrors of their wars, they have grown and deemed corporal punishment in school and home illegal.

The message of this book, examining the corporal punishment of children and questioning this practice, seems to be swimming upstream against centuries of beliefs bound in cultural and religious traditions that are in the conscious and unconscious minds of perhaps the majority of Americans. In fact, if it were not for the circumstances of my life, I may have taken it for granted as well. Therefore I hope the presentation of this book takes into account how deeply enmeshed behaviors and values are difficult to question as well as to discuss.

However, my hope is that perhaps some who read this book may see a possible new way of looking at this issue.

WHAT LESSONS DO AMERICANS STILL NEED TO LEARN?

Irwin Cotler lists seven lessons that should be learned from the Holocaust that are relevant to today's issues.[26] They are:

(1)   The vulnerability of the powerless—Children are the most vulnerable members of our society, and they cannot vote. If they are being punished with paddles in schools in nineteen American states, adults need to stand up for them.

(2)   The responsibility to prevent—We must not allow this paddling in schools, as it sets a tone that the weakest can be

19

beaten while no adult in the United States can, by law, be physically beaten or punished (according to the adults who vote).

(3)   The responsibility to talk to power—Our Congress has ignored two bills to make corporal punishment in schools illegal. At least two physicians on the panel refused to support the bills even though every established medical society in the United States vehemently opposes such punishment based on thirty years of research.

(4)   The danger of silence—Silence from society is deafening.

(5)   The responsibility to educate—Educators in those nineteen states did not educate themselves about the research in front of their noses. No university in the United States either endorses or teaches how, why, or when to use corporal punishment on children.

(6)   The "culture of impunity"—Many of the nineteen states shielded from liability educators who physically punished children.

(7)   The responsibility to remember the lessons–Remembering the lessons is too often not applied to children in schools.

I might also add that we need to learn that if we want corporal punishment to disappear from our landscape, we need to increase the number of children who grow up never having experienced physical punishment.

The nineteen states where school corporal punishment is still legal, according to the Center for Effective Discipline are: Alabama, Arizona, Arkansas, Colorado, Florida, Georgia, Idaho, Indiana, Kansas, Kentucky, Louisiana, Mississippi, Missouri, North Carolina, Oklahoma, South Carolina, Tennessee, Texas, and Wyoming.

As Samuel Chaucer, Holocaust researcher, has observed, "Children need to understand the critical nature of individual rights, generalized tolerance and the immediate accountability of those in power."[27] Maybe then they will protect the next generation of children from being legally beaten in school, to which our generation of adults was blind.

M. Axness, in *Parenting for Peace*, cites research that supports Oliner's contention that ending child corporal punishment raises more altruistic children who are more likely to stand up for the oppressed and less likely to act violently.[28] There is research that points to corporal punishment of children leading to youngsters who are less likely to listen and more likely to be bullies. Although bullying is a major topic in every US state, people do not connect the dots between beating children and later bullying. Children who are hit are more likely to hit their partners and their own children when grown.

THE NEW SCHOOL

Over forty years ago, when I first read Dr. Haim Ginott's statement to parents that children were not for hitting,[29] I was taken aback. Not only was I shocked that someone could challenge the way I was raised—it reverberated in my mind and body—but I also wondered how it could be challenged in such a public manner. Dr. Ginott died too young, when he was in his early fifties. He was a gentle, soft-spoken Israeli with a beard who opposed corporal punishment of children. When he spoke, I felt my body calm itself as though it had a mind of its own, and maybe it did. I learned that in the year of my birth, Ginott's wife-to-be, Alice Cohn, graduated with a PhD from the New School for Social Research in psychology, and she has lived on to carry his message.

The New School was started during the Nazi uprising in the late 1930s when many scholars had to run for their lives. They established a refuge for learning in this lower Manhattan graduate school. Some of the most famous scholars on the subject of the Holocaust were professors in this school. One was Hannah Arendt, who studied the violence in the Nazi era. She had a controversial theory that the violence occurring was more complicated than it appeared on the surface. She discussed the banality of this behavior as ordinary people in Germany seemed to follow orders in droves. They seemed to compartmentalize the violence toward the Jews while being seemingly loving spouses and parents as well as pillars of their communities. To be sure, Arendt had many critics, but she tried to make sense of what appeared to be beyond the scope of human comprehension, although I doubt Hannah Arendt focused much on the rights and welfare of children.

One of Arendt's graduate students, Elizabeth Young-Bruehl, wrote a biography of Arendt and, in 2011, the book *Childism*, which questions how we treat and protect our children in America.[30] She dealt with many aspects of children's rights, including the right enjoyed by all adult citizens: to not be physically hit by teachers and parents. There are many *-isms* in our country, such as sexism, racism, ageism, and anti-Semitism, which are vigorously backed by laws to protect the rights of all citizens in those categories. She argues that children are a class that cannot vote, and lists numerous examples of how children's rights are ignored. She delves into the issue of corporal punishment in school and at home.

IS THE TIDE TURNING AGAINST CORPORAL PUNISHMENT?

In recent years, several prominent American writers have published works arguing that the United States is gradually turning away from corporal punishment of children.

In early spring 2012 at the New School, I saw a public presentation by Dr. Steven Pinker and Dr. Robert J. Lifton[31] . Dr. Pinker just wrote a book, *The Better Angels of Our Nature,* in which he argues that, throughout history, violence, including the Holocaust, has lessened, although there is a long way to go.[32] He discusses how children were subjected over the ages to infanticide, severe beatings, and long hours at dangerous work sites, and were strictly property of their parents or other adults. There has been progress. Pinker describes interesting advertisements from the 1950s in which wives are being spanked by their husbands for such offenses as not brewing a good cup of coffee. Because of laws and public awareness, such advertisements would never be tolerated today. Gradually we are looking at domestic violence and all its tentacles. Hopefully, children will soon receive the same rights as women and all other human beings have to not be physically punished. This sounds like a foreign language, but societies can grow and adapt, and, at least according to Pinker, we are evolving into a less violent society over the long haul. Lifton wrote of the Nazi negative influence on medical doctors and how they too often were compliant in justifying and abetting experiments on the Jews, while living a compartmentalized life where they otherwise lived peaceful lives. Lifton's wife wrote a compassionate biography on Januscz Korczak. The discussions were compelling and reflect how the New School continues to study the importance of the Holocaust topic.

This same belief is reflected in Christopher Boehm's *Moral Origins*, which studies human and animal history in terms of developing a conscience.[33] His studies point to the idea that we are gradually outgrowing the physical punishment answer, which was one of the earliest ways society had to control "improper selfish urges" and behavior. Gradually, there is movement toward internalizing the rules in the context of emotions and reason. Boehm says this is reflected in the changing gene pool, which is slowly moving toward altruism, although there is a long, long way to go.

CHAPTER 3

TOWER OF BABBLE: FROM PARENT BABBLE TO SPANKING BABBLE

L et's get started, parent babble, as John Rosemond (2009), an advocate of spanking, labels the avalanche of research opposing spanking from experts in multiple fields, including neuroscience. We will also look at babble as he calls the clinical experience of the anti-spanking experts. . However, he is a poster child for the swirling, conflicting principles on spanking that he and his fellow pro-spanking colleagues present.[34]

In contrast to many pro-spanking advocates, Rosemond states that the Biblical term *rod* does not mean physical punishment with an implement such as a stick, paddle, or belt. He says the reference to child discipline/punishment is metaphorical and not to be taken literally and that Biblical scholars do not interpret it in that manner. He says, in *fact*, "Why God has not prescribed spanking at all, even with a parent's hand."[35] Somewhere, the pro-spanking advocates of Puritan times are cringing in the "afterlife." Maybe they would believe Rosemond's ideas are parent babble. However, he is strongly pro-spanking and extremely critical of newer alternative theories and practices that do not use spanking. It is his opinion that in the majority of situations, to eliminate the option of spanking would cause ill-behaved and arrogant children. He sees authority to mean spanking should be an option, although some children who go without spanking can grow into well-behaved citizens, while some who are spanked can be indignant and out of control.

SPANKING RULES

Rosemond interprets *rod* to just mean authority. In a statement that could be confusing, he has softened from his stance that spanking should be done in anger to say that it should be done with great emotion.

Rosemond's spanking rules (2009) are that the parent administers it with his or her hand only, the parent's hand makes contact with the rear end only, and the hand strikes the rear no more than three times. He further says that "anything else is a beating," and warns against developing rage by overdoing it. He must have a magic formula that separates acceptable emotional fuel from anger and rage. Dobson and other current pro-spankers, you will see, interpret the Bible and rules of spanking in another language. Although Rosemond is in conflict with many pro-spanking authorities, he determines the definition for parent babble, and his formulas skate by the criteria.[36]

This confusion about spanking rules is exhibited by the recent former Pope Benedict's brother, who has the courage to learn from painful experience in the context of the German culture where Hitler's lieutenants restarted legal corporal punishment in schools.

The pope's brother learned from painful experience and scientific research that corporal punishment in schools is destructive. George Ratzinger, an educator, said, "I was happy to learn corporal punishment in schools was made illegal [in Germany] in 1980." He said that he used corporal punishment and "had a bad conscience" about it and was sorry for all the pain caused and the situations with children that worsened.[37] In his earlier crisis of conscience, he did not report to others the sexual abuse of students, of which he was aware as well. He said, as if it is true for everyone, "of course today one condemns such actions" (Eddy, Rizzo, 2010). His assumption that his insights are commonly accepted proved to be premature—to say the least!

When I started working for the Philadelphia Department of Human Services, the first thing I learned (from supervisors with twenty to thirty years of experience) was to keep from instructing a parent about techniques, no matter how seemingly gentle, to hit with an open hand on the backside or spank their kids, as any form of permission can be interpreted as a license to beat children. The bulk of the clients were not severe abusers. In my thirty-two years as a social worker, supervisor, administrator, foster home finder, and trainer, the majority of family reports were either deemed to be unsubstantiated or were referred to Services to Children in their Own Homes (SCOH). We also educated foster parent applicants and ongoing foster parents in positive child discipline techniques. In all situations, we had to utilize tested techniques for nonphysical discipline of children and, if needed, to send them to therapeutic experts in those skills.

There is the rule of "no marks," at which too many parents become expert. For instance, I worked with a disabled child whose parent wrapped a towel around a pipe to beat him and keep marks from showing. It was not until there were internal injuries that the abuse was noticed. Kagan wrote about this, as it is seen quite a bit.[38] I learned so much that changed the way I had been programmed about corporal punishment of children. I had no preformed idea that there was a Biblical dictate to hit children.

In contrast to the "no marks" proponents are people such as Michael Pearl and Debi Pearl of No Greater Joy Ministries in Butte, Montana, which has quite a following. According to the Pearls, you can advocate your divine duty to correct children, and it is okay to hit them with a plumbing tube as early as six months of age.[39] Oh, by the way, a number of their followers have severely beaten their children with that tube and lost control in the process, killing a few. Pearl compares training a child to training a mule. This is not the last animal/child-rearing comparison you will see in the book. The Pearls deny teaching corporal punishment but advocate "controlled application of a spanking implement."

Other religious leaders have different rules. J. Dobson advocates use of an implement (usually a switch) until there is pain, or there will be no gain from the punishment.[40]

As mentioned above, Rosemond (2006) says to use your hand and not an implement. They have different rules about at which ages a child may be hit. Dobson wants parents to wait until eighteen months. To add to this, he says not to hit children who are too rebellious, such as those with oppositional defiant disorder, as it only makes them worse. He says not to hit compliant children who will obey without a fight. He compares training children to the way he trained his dog. Few appear to pay attention to these recommendations, however, as "too many" parents use some sort of physical punishment on babies anyway. They and the two-year-olds receive a lion's share of the injuries and even loss of life from these practices. Even when young children are not severely injured, parents who have negative relationships, including physical roughness from the early months, promote more aggressive children and set up a spiraling use of punishment.[41]

Although Dobson (2003) is pro-spanking, he admits physical punishment could be dangerous in combination with a laundry list of parental and child characteristics. Parents should not have substance abuse issues or alcohol dependence, engage in domestic violence at home, have mental health issues or anger management issues, have been from abusive homes, or be "whimsical" about spanking children. Children should not be physically disabled or have significant mental health issues. It seems somewhere between two and ten is the most appropriate time to use physical punishment, according to Dobson. Teens should not be spanked, partially because they won't listen and are big enough to hit back. To his partial credit, Dobson warns of widespread child abuse and misuse of punishment and warns people to be careful but to cause some pain. Oh, by the way, Dobson is in favor of school paddling, although he must know how ominous a task it is for educators to be screened for the variables mentioned above and to really know the children's physical, emotional, and family histories.

For years I have been a "groupie" at Barnes and Noble stores and the late, great Borders chain, as well as Strand Bookstore in New York, among many others. I have examined their books on psychology, parenting, and child behavior countless times over the years, and the most enduring books on their bookshelves are by Dobson. The others' shelf lives are so much shorter.

A DIFFERENT INTERPRETATION
OF "SPARING THE ROD"

Child psychologist Thomas Phelan (2007), in *123 Magic for Christian Parents: Effective Discipline for Children 2–12*, says: "Let's face up to reality: ninety-nine percent of all spankings are parental temper tantrums. They are simply the outbursts of parents who have lost control, don't know what to do and want revenge by inflicting pain. Parents who have big problems with self control and anger management try to justify and rationalize spanking by saying 'you have to set limits, it's for their own good, and having to hurt kids hurts me more than it does them.'" Furthermore, he has another interpretation of the Bible:

> But doesn't the Bible teach you if you spare the rod you will spoil the child? The verse in question is Proverbs 13:24. The Amplified version put it this way: "He who spares the rod (of discipline) hates his son, but he who loves him disciplines diligently and punishes him early." The emphasis in this verse is less on the method of discipline and more of an admonition to discipline. Consider a similar verse. "Discipline your son and he will give you peace; he will bring delight into your soul." Again the Bible is emphasizing the wisdom of discipline, not necessarily the use of corporal punishment (Proverbs 29:17).[42]

He states that the 1, 2, 3 plan will eliminate the need for hitting. This plan teaches parents techniques to diffuse their anger and then rather than lengthy lecturing, briefly discussing the behavior to be stopped using a counting technique to be followed by a time out if the child does not respond. It is examined in much greater detail in his book.

THE INGRAINED TRADITION OF SPANKING

In my hands-on experience working with foster parents in training, I found that many of them are so indoctrinated by tradition and these "experts" that they would vehemently challenge me in training classes, saying that spanking is necessary even for children who come into care from previous abuse. If they do not modify these views, they cannot be accepted as foster parents.

When you have judges who try child abuse cases but secretly beat their own disabled children with leather belts and minimize how serious it was, you know that the education is for professionals, not just parents. Such a judge is in Texas, one of the nineteen states that allow physical discipline of children in schools. More about him is forthcoming.

As mentioned above, Pope Benedict's brother renounced the practice of school corporal punishment after administering it himself for a number of years. The pope himself grew out of adverse experiences. He, at age fourteen, was ordered into the Hitler Youth Program that was in his native Poland. However, a couple of years later, he went AWOL from the program, and the Germans were looking for him and other deserters to put them to death, but he escaped.

One reason corporal punishment is so accepted at home and school by Christians is because of their belief in original sin. Murray Straus, in *Beating the Devil Out of Them,* discusses this historical fact.[43] Conservative Christian John Wesley believed that children must have their wills sacrificed in the name of obeying their parents at every turn. Wesley believed in hitting babies if they even showed a spark of independence. Children were born evil, and only the proper training could aid them with this malady.

In contrast, Jews do not believe in eternal punishment or original sin I was impressed by Rabbi Schmuely Boteach's work arguing the position of the majority of Jews arguing children are not born evil. He was so respectful that those who disagreed, such as Pat Boone and Glenn Beck, were willing to give Boteach's position some thought. He writes about it in his book *Kosher Jesus*. I hope that I have the skills to show respect for other positions, and to have others give my ideas a fair hearing.[44]

The innocent children and babies slaughtered in the Holocaust, I fervently believe, were not born evil. In fact, the most abused children who are killed by their parents in the United States are under one year of age. With substance abuse, alcoholism, domestic violence, severe mental health issues, and anger management issues so rampant in society, it seems hardly kosher to blame the children for being "born evil" and in need of following their too-often perpetrator parents' wills at all costs.

The field of epi-genetics addresses this issue. This field studies how genetic predisposition affects their environments. Children are born with differing temperaments, and interaction does have an impact on how behavior will express itself.

Consider the following quotation by Dr. Margaret McHugh: "Doctors, especially young doctors, want to believe that parents only beat older children. I have to keep telling them, no, they beat their babies." [45]

John Callahan (1992) is a quadriplegic cartoonist who was spanked and beaten from his earliest recollections. He has cartoons of a father threatening the embryos in his pregnant wife's stomach, telling them that they must stop misbehaving or he will beat them.[46] At first I cringed when I saw that cartoon. But with further research into how babies have been treated in history, I realized that, unfortunately, this cartoon was not as farfetched as one might imagine: "Research on parental behavior in the US shows that 75% of parents smack their one year olds."[47]

Many of our books on babies deal directly with concerns about parents hitting babies. H. Karp (2002), in *The Happiest Baby on the Block.* has a section titled "Don't Rock the Cradle Too Hard: Babies' Frustrations and Child Abuse." Murkoff and Mazel (2010), in the ten-month-old child section of their book *What to Expect the First Year,* have a huge section on to spank or not to spank. It is evident they know what to expect the first year: that too many parents will spank their little babies. Brown and Fields (2011) in *Baby 411* state specifically not to spank. In *Superbaby,* Berman (2010) implores parents not to spank babies, as it spikes their levels of cortisol, which can kill brain cells and slow brain growth. Azrin (1986), perhaps the foremost, earliest behaviorist in toilet training, in his book *Toilet Training in One Day,* talks about the damage parents do when they spank the littlest ones during toilet training, causing terror but no learning. I saw countless parents spank babies younger than one year old when they soiled or wet themselves.

We have a long history of underestimating a child's pain from the earliest infancy, noted by those who studied the history of surgery in children. For example, R. Scaer describes how insufficient anesthesia was used in operations on children as recently as a couple of decades ago, as even medical experts grossly underestimated pain in children.[48]

I propose that the powerful pro-physical punishment tradition in this country follows this path of minimizing children's physical and emotional pain. Furthermore, studies show how these painful rites of childhood affect people over life in physical and emotional illness. Therefore, many professionals in the medical community, are also underestimating this effect on adults.

Sir Hiram Stevens Maxim, lived from 1840 to 1916, he was a man who did not believe in original sin and was an inventor of many original products, such as smokeless gunpowder. He was spontaneous, creative, physically imposing, and did not believe in corporal punishment in any *way*, shape, or form. When his son's behavior did not respond to his wife's paddling, she pleaded with him to use physical punishment with him. Her *son's* biography of his father bears out this story.[49] When I saw the movie about Sir Hiram Stevens Maxim, I did not originally believe that this man went to great lengths not to hit his son despite his wife and relatives badgering him to do so. He stopped the badgering by taking his son out to cut branches to be used as switches. They cut down several to find an appropriate one for a potential stinging sensation. Then Maxim alone went with the child to his room. There he tested out the switch and other implements by hitting them on the bed. He found the right one and had his son beat the bed loudly for an extended period. His wife thought he might be going too far as she heard the "beating going on for an agonizing length," and she rushed upstairs to stop it and hugged the child. After that, the mother no longer insisted on spanking, as the father had broken his power struggle with her. The son was so amazed and dazzled by his father's inventive way to handle this disagreement without raising a hand to him that he remembered this loving act for the rest of his life. It was so stunning that it was included in a major movie about his father's life. If only we could all learn from such brilliant lessons.

Prolific researcher Bruce Perry, one of the world's top experts on the effect of child maltreatment on the developing brain, states that spanking is not conducive to a child's health. "Needless to say spanking or any other form of harsh discipline does not and cannot encourage empathy..." He said "needless to say," but obviously it must be said.

"To encourage empathy, discipline by reasoning, by perspective taking, consistency of appropriate consequences, and, above all, love" shows that children who receive corporal punishment are more aggressive, more likely to be antisocial as teenagers, and even have lower IQs than those who are not physically disciplined.[50]

The rules on when to spank take a detour around toilet training. Consider this quote from Rosemond (2012) in *Toilet Training without Tantrums*: "First, the friend who told you to spank gave you very bad advice. That seemed to work, I know, but bedwetting is not a disciplinary issue."[51] Furthermore, John Rosemond says, toilet training is not the occasion for a spanking, as there are specific steps that he plots out that can stop rebellion against being toilet trained. Just as he found alternatives to spanking for bedwetting and soiling, other professionals and parents have come up with alternatives for spanking that work in all situations if the parent understands child development, the effect of harsh punishment on a child, and anger.

ANGER

Countless theories and books discuss in different terms just what anger is. People who have been abused themselves can displace anger, as can people dealing with the stress of life's challenges, which may include poverty and frustration. Different schools of psychology will tell you that you can be angry and not realize it: "But do we really recognize the full spectrum of the anger response... and how many of us can really recognize the details of our own anger response?"[52]

The research on anger has grown significantly through the blossoming interest in neuroscience and its incorporation into research. We will see that this helps explain how we all have variations in our recognition of rage and anger. Joseph Shrand, MD, points out some of the factors involved. in a Harvard Medical School publication, For example, we all differ in our ability to "process anger." This depends on environmental experiences and genetic factors and how they interact. According to Shrand, "We are not born with the ability to monitor our anger response or to 'take it down a notch.'"[53]

Three scientists at the University of Delaware studied anger in 257 eight-year-old students. They found that there are at least five types of anger experienced by children, depending on their heredity and environmental factors.[54] This depends on the degree of "physiological arousal" and how much control they have over this reaction. Telling parents to spank when not angry is complicated by the complexity of the issue.

The prefrontal cortex, PFC, develops at different rates. When it is fully and appropriately developed, people have the ability to challenge and control their anger. In children, it is just beginning to

36

mature, and adults vary on the degree that it does mature. People think they have control, but our reactions are often tied to the history of experiences and genetics that our limbic systems endure.

In fact, we do not always recognize that we get angrier at others who appear different or more vulnerable. University of Miami researchers studied 1,006 teens with acne. They experienced much more bullying when they had active acne. The anger display subsided as the acne healed. "Acne is just one of a myriad of examples of how we mistakenly misjudge a person's character," according to the researchers.[55]

Justification for the use of physical force to correct children is an example of the attitude "science be damned." One reason numerous researchers and theorists see as a contributor to violence is that people tend to dehumanize the "other" individual or group that they focus on as targets. Therefore, the belief that children are born evil, which bubbles beneath the surface of our culture's traditions in punitive child rearing from its Puritanical history, facilitates and often exacerbates the punishment and its justification. Felicity DeZulueta, in her book *From Pain to Violence: The Traumatic Roots of Destructiveness*, discusses depersonalization as a major factor that fuels such behavior. By reducing the humanity of others, such as children who have not yet been "physically broken of their will," a green light is given for physical punishment as necessary.[56]

Jewish Pastoral Care is a field that is growing as religious leaders gain more knowledge of human behavior patterns and research. There is a growing awareness of domestic violence and how it affects children who see it, hear it, or sense it in their homes. Dayle A. Friedman has done research demonstrating the high degree of physical abuse that occurs to children when they live in homes where there is domestic violence and teachers are not aware of the violence.[57]

Studies demonstrate that having struggling parents read about more positive ways of disciplining children results in gradual improvement. For example, researchers have shown that Early Head Start programs and parenting classes reduce by 30 percent the use of physical discipline by parents who were already using corporal punishment on babies and toddlers. And when parents learned about child development, they used up to 35 percent less physical discipline when their children were a year older, as parents reduced the use of corporal punishment by 7 percent for each year older they became[58]

IN THE TALMUD CHAPTER

Many people who strike their children do so not because they are evil or mean but because they believe they are doing *God's* will. They often cite the phrase in Proverbs, "He who spares the rod hates his *son.*" The problem is that pulling one line out of the Bible ignores the rest of the text. Much of the Book of Proverbs is filled with good counsel on how to be a better person. In Chapter 22, we are taught, "Train a child in the way he should behave and even when he is old he will not depart from it." Isn't it possible that the rod Proverbs refers to is to be used to point out lessons of skillful firmness? When we fail to properly educate our children, we not only spoil them; we show them the opposite of love. We must use the rod to point out right and wrong, not to beat our children into submission the way slaves have been treated throughout history.

When taken in its entirety, Judaism can hardly sanction the use of violence against children. Even the famous sentence in

Deuteronomy to stone the stubborn, rebellious son to death was, according to the Talmud, never carried out. This recommendation isn't taken literally. Instead, while discipline was and is still crucial for raising healthy children, striking a child need never occur. The Talmud suggests, "A child should be pushed aside with the left hand, and drawn closer with the right,"[59] according to Rabbi Larry Kaplan. Although Rabbi Kaplan, who is quoted by child protection agencies, is opposed to corporal punishment of children, some of the more Orthodox Jewish groups disagree with his recommendations. Therefore, in my opinion, it is remarkable that the state of Israel, which has a large Orthodox base, was able to establish laws banning child corporal punishment in schools but not in the family. There is a saying that if there are two Jews, there are three opinions; however, there is also a love of learning about the latest research and protection of its most valuable and vulnerable: the children.

America's most devout Christian organizations revere many of Israel's ideologies and its love of democracy, but this reverence often stops cold at issues related to disciplining children and the Christian belief that children are born with original sin and need to have punishment, including physical punishment, to break their will. While a larger segment of the Christian religions in America are less intense and more flexible about child discipline techniques, the patterns for generations of corporal punishment and spanking are alive and well (if you call that well) in the United States.

Joseph Telushkin, a prolific and respected author, has written a book that explains some of the fundamental differences in attitudes that Jews and Christians have about corporal punishment.

In *The Book on Jewish Values*, he sets out 365 daily principles to elevate the spiritual and practical actions of Jews and to ensure the best chance for the next generations. On day 135 of the year of rethinking values and actions, his excerpt is titled "Don't Threaten Your Child with Physical Punishment."[60] This learned man encapsulates the thinking behind Israel's banning corporal punishment for children in school and home as well. (He cites the Babylonian Talmud, where the rabbis advise, "If you must strike a child, hit him only with a shoelace.") On day 355, he has a chapter concerning "A Law That Needs to Be Changed." He states that one of the reasons that teachers still hit learning disabled children, who have been receiving a scourge of physical punishment at home as well as in school, was that Maimonides, a great, caring Jewish scholar of nearly a thousand years ago, who was in most ways as humane as humane can be, endorsed corporal punishment and that teachers and parents have used that as a partial justification for physically punishing children. As mentioned, the Jews read (the people of the book) and study research and are flexible enough to grow and change, challenging respected scholars of the past. Israel's decision to ban corporal punishment of children at school demonstrates the power of the Jewish love of book learning, and the result is a respect for children's rights learned from Holocaust studies as well.

The Orthodox community in the United States knows that American laws can place children in other homes to protect them from corporal punishment, and this may be partially the reason the Orthodox are ambivalent about reporting maltreatment of children outside the community. This extends to sexual abuse as well. There has been some progress in this area, but their willingness to change has been painfully slow. This is also partially happening because, in the past centuries, the non- Jewish civil authorities in places such as Europe unfairly treated the Jews in the civil court system. Old habits die hard, even at the expense of children's safety. The Jews have a precedent that even the strictest rules for following the high holy days and the Sabbath are superseded by realistic health and safety concerns. As I study Jewish ethics, I am returning to a renewed respect for my heritage and the manner in which they evolved in the treatment of children in the real world.

Although it is not legal for children in Israel to be hit in school or at home, apparently in the cocoon of extreme Orthodox education this can still take place. William Kolbrenner, a professor of English at Bar-Ilan University, changed schools for his five-year-old since the rabbi who was the principal of his son's school believed in and carried out corporal punishment on children. The rabbi considered his manner of punishment a benefit to children. The rabbi said his son would miss the "potches"—which are smacks and spanking given "cute" Yiddish terminology.[61] Kolbrenner (2012) points out that although corporal punishment in New York City schools is illegal, the ultraorthodox find a way within their insular tradition to keep it going in their religious schools as well.

Kolbrenner is insightful about the difficult nature of separating adult frustrations and unresolved life issues from being expressed by physically punishing children. He knows of college graduates who moved back to Flatbush or Bora Park from Ivy League schools who became increasingly physical in their punishment of their children, as it was accepted more in the culture they had learned as children. He wanted to tell the rabbi, "On a day that you are not angry at your wife; not upset with your kids; not frustrated by work;

not with a bank overdraft, please feel free to patch away, but otherwise keep your hands off my son." He had the resources to change his son's school rather than having to say these words to the rabbi.

In the nineteen states where corporal punishment is legal, countless families are not in a position financially or otherwise; they are at the mercy of teachers who are quite human and may have an addiction to food, alcohol, or drugs; may endure domestic violence at home; or may have mental illness, anger management issues, a history of being abused as a child, financial problems, or a lack of education about the mountain of research on the serious effects of physically punishing children who themselves may have been abused at home or are autistic or disabled.

CATHOLIC SCHOOLS

Other religions such as Catholicism demonstrate conflicting opinions about child corporal punishment. Here are two different views. The first is from Archbishop Gregory Aymond: "I do not believe the teachings of the Catholic Church as we interpret them condone corporal punishment. It's hard for me to imagine in any shape or form Jesus using a paddle."[62] The second is from Robert Lazarlere, who is a director of psychology at Father Flanagan's Boys Home, and publicly advocates that corporal punishment of children should not be stopped.

"It is virtually unheard, moreover, for school personnel, to be required beforehand to demonstrate any competence at hitting safely and judiciously, to have their paddles inspected and held to any standards of size, weight, composition, or craftsmanship, and least of all to have the velocity of their swings measured.[63]

"Thus we can reasonably expect that paddlers will hit harder than they intend to or in some cases, hit parts of the body that they didn't intend to."

SPANKING CHILDREN WITH AUTISM AND ORPHANS

Matthew Israel, Harvard-trained therapist, specialized in work with children and young adults with autism. He carefully trained his aides to spank these young people in a "controlled way," but the children moved so much that many were injured. He then resorted to electrical shock as a punishment. This occurred although his legendary mentor, B.F. Skinner, rated as the top behaviorist in the field, was opposed to hitting children for scientific behavioral reasons. Why didn't Israel learn from his mentor? At the time of this writing his school for special children still uses shocks.

Like children with disabilities, orphans have often been targets of corporal punishment. Unfortunately, in recent years, some "orphans" from foreign countries placed in the United States received physical punishment that severely injured and even killed them. This ruined the hope that they would be saved by giving them loving Christian homes as opposed to living with the poverty and chaos and war of their previous countries. As described previously, the reason this occurred was often that the conservative Christian Biblical principles call for corporal punishment of children as necessary to remove the original sin that they had from birth.[64] Many children were also sent back with little warning.

As discussed, the Pearls (1997), who sold more than *700,000* books to devotees on training children,, recommended that children be corrected early, even as babies, and suggested hitting them with a plumbing implement that had a flexible but firm plastic tubing. Some of the orphans were "corrected" and thrashed with this tube in such a manner leading to injuries and deaths that occurred. Upon hearing this, third world countries protested. There were also protests from Russia, as some of the children adopted from their territories were seriously injured, killed, or sent back to them with notes blaming the children for the caretakers giving up on them.

Another example of mistreatment of orphans, according to Joyce (2013), involved Sam Allison, a house painter from Tennessee who worked relentlessly with these adoptee orphans for hours, and if they complained he would hit them. Not much was done, as the conservative Christian church is dominant and has powerful political sway. In fact, a Tennessee child protection worker said, according to Joyce, that the Tennessee Children's Services was unduly silenced and influenced in their investigation by the right-wing community.

Joyce presents a multitude of examples in which children's rights, if they had any, as well as their safety, were trampled on during this wave of adoption of third world children that was supported by some of the most powerful church leaders and icons in the United States.

Clearly, the many languages of US pro-spanking babble can extend across the ocean as well as at home to the international detriment of children.

CHAPTER 4

CAPTAIN KANGAROO, OTHER ANIMALS, AND CORPORAL PUNISHMENT

The Nazis banned Jews from keeping pets, and while they brutalized Jews, they sought to protect animals. In fact, there is a cartoon of animals saluting a Nazi leader. In other words, the Nazis who butchered Jewish children often treated animals better. We will see how animals in the United States had legal protections against abuse before children in this chapter.

Let us examine the parallels between child corporal punishment and cruelty to animals. In the United States today, there is some of the same ambivalence about physically punishing pets and physically punishing children.

On the one hand, many Americans believe that it is wrong to physically punish an animal. For example, Victoria Schade, a host with Animal Planet, and a certified pet trainer who produced an award-winning dog training video says, "I'll say it clearly and without embellishment: Physical punishment has no place in your relationship with your dog...hitting a dog with a newspaper in potty training only makes the dog afraid of the newspaper itself and you, but teaches nothing."[65]

Another dog trainer who has come out strongly against hitting dogs is Tamar Gellar, who was an intelligence officer with the Israeli army. She wrote a book on how she was beaten at home and only through seeing a psychiatrist was able to move forward with her life. Her incredibly loving and gentle grandmother was the rock that held her together. She saw military dogs beaten and isolated, which taught them aggression. She bonded with animals and learned not to hit them no matter what the challenge. She became a dog trainer for individuals and organizations, including the wealthy and Hollywood types. She wrote *The Loved Dog: The Playful Nonaggressive Way to Teach Your Dog Good Behavior.*[66]

This is also the opinion of the horse whisperers (specialized trainers) on how to treat these animals without physically punishing them. Numerous books and movies demonstrate their skills.

Some elephant trainers, too, are against physical punishment of the animals they work with. In Tennessee, an elephant inadvertently crushed a man. Its trainers refused to use physical punishment on the elephant and instead used a positive behavioral/reinforcement model to change the elephant's future behavior.

In contrast to people who advocate against hitting animals, some people believe that it is necessary. For example, pro-spanker James Dobson compared training children to the physical punishment he gave his dog. And the Pearls (1997), who believe in hitting children early and often with a plumbing implement, compare correcting children to how one would correct a mule.

In fact, animals have had more protection against physical punishment than children have in the United States for over a century. In the 1900s, there were no laws to protect children from any level of physical punishment. When a young lady known as Mary Ellen was being seriously beaten by her family, there was no agency to call charged with protecting her. Only the SPCA, which protected animals, covered sheltering living beings from abuse. Persistent folks had the government allow the SPCA to protect Mary Ellen and remove her from danger.[67]

WHAT ANIMAL LOVERS CAN TEACH US ABOUT RAISING CHILDREN WITHOUT PUNISHMENT

Tracey Hogg (2013), in *Secrets of the Toddler Whisperer*, following in the tradition of horse whisperers, discusses methods of raising children without physical punishment. She recommends twelve steps:[68]

1. Know your boundaries and set rules.
2. Look at your own behavior to see what you are teaching the child.
3. Listen to yourself to make sure that you are in charge, not the toddler.
4. Wherever possible, plan ahead.
5. Avoid difficult settings or circumstances.
6. See the situation through your eyes.
7. Pick your battles.
8. Offer closed-end choices.
9. *Don't* be afraid to say no.

10.   Praise good behavior and correct or ignore bad.

11.   *Don't* rely on corporal punishment.

12.   Remember that giving in does not equal love.

Bruce Perry (Perry, Szalavitz, 2006), renowned neuroscientist, wrote the book *The Boy Raised as a Dog* about a boy who was treated horribly in childhood and subsequently had serious trouble developing empathy. In his book *Born for Love*, he recommends against spanking and corporal punishment of children, as it may well interfere with the ability to develop empathy. Adding support to Perry's belief are the results of a study in which C.B.Flynn found that when fathers used corporal punishment on their sons, the sons were in turn cruel to animals.[69] PETA, be advised.

Finally, world-famous television star Bob Keeshan, known as Captain Kangaroo, lived up to his stage name by discussing how children should never receive corporal punishment in school. "A kangaroo is an animal, isn't it?" he stated in a lengthy piece in *The Humanist* in 1988.[70]

"Despite the fact that our Constitution protects religious freedoms of all of us by separating church and *state,* we find some referring to religious dogma to justify public policy," Keeshan said. He further stated that "He that spareth the rod hateth his son" was attributed to King Solomon, who was a failed parent and violent ruler in the Proverbs of the Old Testament. Keeshan stated that teachers were poorly trained, and it would take money to properly teach them the new methods of behavior modification. Since 1988, a mountain of research further justifies Keeshan's advocacy, and countless techniques have been developed for teachers to avoid hitting their students.

METAPHORIC ANIMALS

Horses: A prolific scholar on the brain, L. Cozolino has suggested, "Just like the saying 'Let's link horse sense to horsepower,' let us say lets link horse sense to parenting."[71] In *The Social Neuroscience of Education*, he discusses the need for teachers and parents to be "amygdala whisperers" just like the horse whisperers and toddler whisperers we discussed. (The amygdala is discussed in chapter 7.)Cozolino recommends using this whispering with troubled students who are hurt and angry, precisely the ones, along with autistic and minority children, who receive the bulk of the paddling in the nineteen states. "With these students, teachers need to become amygdala whisperers by using warmth, emphatic caring. And positive regard to decrease amygdala activation and create a state-of mind that increases neuro-plasticity and learning." Cozolino points out that the amygdala, when under a state of perceived danger or fear, sets the body and mind into "let's live for today (often recklessly) and not worry about the future" mode. This is reminiscent of the need to develop delay of gratification, which children reared in a more peaceful manner are more likely to have.

Cobras and Pit Bulls: Domestic violence is often linked with physical abuse of children. Gottman and Jacobson use animal metaphors to discuss two types of perpetrators.[72] The cobra type of perpetrator can be calm while battering his wife or abusing the child. Blood pressure and heart rate go down as the anger, which he does not recognize, increases. The cobras often manipulate social workers, judges, and police as they remain calm and never blame themselves for the abuse. The cobra is much more resistant to therapy than the pit bull. The pit bull is not calm, and, during rages, his blood pressure and heart rate go up. He is aware to a greater degree of his body sensations, and recognizes it as anger. The violence can be severe, but he feels superior to the law and the victims. While the pit bull feels down and depressed, he often blames others. To counterbalance, the cobra is the more dangerous as he lashes out while calm and feels above the chaos he has caused.

Telling cobras never to be angry before they spank a child is not a plan, as they do not connect anger as a contributing factor. So the approach by pro-spankers of telling these parents to control their rage would not begin to work with these men who are so artful at conning even professionals. The pit bulls may be more likely to recognize their anger but are unlikely to calm down enough to slow down and stop the physical maltreatment of their wife or children.

Pro-spankers are taking a major risk by giving permission to parents to spank and giving their conflicting cookbook advice on spanking etiquette. Anger is a complex subject that is continually being researched and has different meanings for various persons.[73]

John Gottman and Neil Jacobson (2011) have done voluminous research on married couples and found that in those relationships where "horsemen" contempt, stonewalling, criticism, and defensiveness are noticed frequently by researchers, these marriages are more likely to end in divorce. John Gottman is not just talking about domestic violence and pit bulls and cobras when he is opposed to corporal punishment of children. He has studied the methods of working toward stopping domestic violence, which is detrimental to the children, both because they witness the behavior and because they are more often physically beaten than other children. He points out that studies show that when parents learn alternatives to spanking, they "drop the spanking." According to research, children who have been spanked more often are aggressive.

Clifton B. Flynn's study finding that spanked children often abuse animals again shows how corporal punishment can lead to a variety of destructive behaviors. The use of the word *horseman* to describe contempt appears to be another "animal" reference that is apt.

CHAPTER 5

MY STORY ISN'T UNBEATABLE

Consider my mother's end-of-life words written about my brother:

When you were a toddler you knocked a lamp over. I thought it was the right thing to spank you. After that you were not feeling well and when you got out of bed you were overactive. A cycle began. You got into things and I spanked hard. It was really not discipline…You were a target, even though I loved you very much and still love you.

My mother was terrified of the law and likely would have followed it. Breaking even the slightest legal mandate was not her style, but there was and still is no law about physically punishing your children that much of the world has adopted.

I kept after you to do things my way. I did not know enough to know that was breaking your spirit. I did the same to Dave.

My brother was placed outside of the home for several years, as he did not respond to spanking, and my parents had precious few other tools. I was terrified of challenging my parents and have spent about forty years of my life in therapy. I did not know why my brother and I spent our lives in careers in child protective services. At first I did not know why I was working as an advocate to challenge laws not protecting children from physical punishment after I retired.

My mother had lost her own mom at four and remembers adults dismissing her need to be comforted. During her mother's funeral, she was left to wander by herself in the cemetery while others participated in the ceremony. For over eighty years, she remembered this experience. She also remembers her mother offering her a candy bar at age three and refusing to accept it, and she felt guilty about it for eighty years. She lost her father when she was barely a teenager and had a stepmother whom she described as not treating her well, and in a letter we found, she described her as wacky.

She had little experience of warm, supportive parenting and accepted the cultural norm of spanking my brother and me as gospel. She spent much of her eighty years lamenting this treatment of her children. She died in September 2013, two months shy of ninety-three years of age.

When I was eleven, my mother strongly recommended that I go to therapy, in part to tell the therapist that she was not such a bad mother to my brother, who had come back from placement and was better but not "calm enough" for my parents' needs. I had every intention of protecting my mother as I always had dutifully done. A funny thing happened when I came to the therapist. I broke down and cried. My therapist was also my dad's therapist, and, Dr Seymour Siegel was also an orphan. He knew about the issues. Dads and moms respecting each other and protecting children is part of the role modeling needed. There were pamphlets in the office about moms and dads who were calmer than my parents were. This was an eye opener.

As a therapist myself, I usually quickly learned how a child was disciplined by asking, "What did your parents do when they were angry?" A large portion of clients discussed all types of physical punishment, and, on occasion, neglect. They did not realize how this punishment had stayed with them just under their conscious radar. They at first vehemently defended their parents, but many later were able to see the effects that lingered.

I had some clients who outwardly appeared angry and rebellious, but as the onion skin of their past histories opened to deeper parts of their past relationships, I saw many of these clients break down and cry about the lack of safety in their childhoods that was often intertwined with physical discipline.

THE LASTING EFFECTS OF CRUELTY TO ORPHANS

My father vowed never to go to another institution again as long as he lived. He had endured a very painful existence in an orphanage. At age eighty-seven, he became so ill that he could not move or control many of his bodily functions. My elderly mother could not care for him and was overwhelmed. He was placed in a nursing home and died within a few days, which was much quicker than anyone, including the doctors, expected. This was devastating to my family, as the legacy of his orphanage had another defining event.

Both my brother and I became social workers for abused and neglected children. I guess our career choices were part of these aftershocks. This was also the case for my father's long-time (twenty-five years) therapist, Dr. Seymour Siegel, who wrote a book, *An Orphan in New York*, in which he describes his childhood experiences in the Hebrew Orphan Asylum of New York. He describes his first day as overwhelming, which turned to terror when the children were ordered to stand still. One did not, and the man with the powerful voice strode over to him and slapped him so hard that the child fell down. He describes the "subsequent abuse in that environment" in his book. "I wept within myself, and there was no adult at the institution to comfort me, not the first day or the last." Dr. Siegel got the counseling and help he needed not long after leaving the institution and received a master's of social work from Case Western Reserve University and a doctorate from the University of Pennsylvania. He was a therapist and director of Jewish Family Services in Camden, New Jersey, taught at Rutgers, and served on various boards. My father did not get any counseling until much later in his life, and Dr. Siegel kept my father and family afloat with years of therapy, individual and family.

The US Bureau of the Census in 1900 listed children in the Home for Hebrew Orphans in Philadelphia as "inmates." I did not want to use the word *inmate* without some extra research; however, I found that Jewish orphanages in New York, St. Louis, New Orleans, and as far away as South Africa used this term for orphans until at least 1920. My father was placed in this orphanage several years later, after his father, an Orthodox rabbi who traveled the country performing ceremonies and filling in as a leader in congregations, died in Salt Lake City and was buried there. My father's mom was unable to care for the six children left behind. Two of her sons, Abe and Joe, were placed in this orphanage on South Street in Philadelphia. It was common in those days for orphanages to take in children with one overwhelmed parent. The other siblings were more fortunate and were raised by relatives. My dad and brother Joe ran away from the orphanage but the inmates were caught.

In *History of the Jewish Foster Home and Orphan Asylum in Philadelphia*, Fleischman documents the numerous charities and philanthropists that worked to set up the orphanages in Philadelphia, which included some of the luminaries of that era, such as Rebecca Gratz and Dr. Solis Cohen.[74] There were ceremonies and dedications and platitudes given about the importance of caring for children. But corporal punishment was assumed to be a viable disciplinary method..

His orphanage experience left him terrified of authority figures and of breaking any rules. He followed rules and laws to the extreme. He drove his car well below the speed limit even if he was alone on the road. This practice frustrated his passengers and cars following him as well. My brother once wrote a harmless poem about how boring my hometown was called "Hemmed in Camden (NJ)." Abe Cooperson, an orphan who had tried to run away from the Hebrew Home at age seven, feared that officials from Camden might find out and pleaded with us not to let the public see it. At his job as a life insurance salesperson, he would tell customers if another company had a better policy. He survived as he was assigned to the poorest clients; he often took me to their homes, and I met their families. He would give them toys that belonged to my brother and me even before we were done using them.

One thing my father knew was not against the law was physically punishing children. He was mild-mannered in almost every way but would resort to hitting me with his hands or a belt, as he had not learned any other method of disciplining children. He in many ways would be kind and empathetic but not in laying down the home rules. If it was against the law, my father (if he followed his other behaviors), would not have hit me, and, I surmise, may have had incentive to learn other discipline techniques. He was muscular and did not know his own strength.

Those "spankings" with hands/and or belts left me terrified, and I turned my feelings inward. My older brother, who was more rebellious than I, would fight back and even laugh at the attempts at setting limits. This frustrated my parents so much that they had him go to therapy at Philadelphia Child Guidance Clinic and had the State of New Jersey involved. He wound up being placed out of home for a year and a half. Is it an accident that my brother followed my father's history of placement with his own? As for me, I was terrified to ever stand up to my parents, as my brother was an example of what happens when you didn't follow a "perfect" path of compliance.

I remember the expression on my brother's face when he was placed. He tried to smile, but I could read between the lines and saw that, beneath this façade, he was crying and in great pain. I would see that expression again on his face after he was drafted and ready to board the plane to be shipped out. Dan was taken to the Children's Home in Allaire, New Jersey, in about 1954. He was crying and upset when he moved. He was terrified about the separation. The superintendent of this institution beat my brother's head and body to quiet him. He was a bit like Dr. Bruno Bettelheim, who escaped the Nazis and opened up a famous group home for youth who were neglected and abused. Bettelheim was considered a pioneer in how to best calmly set limits for children and teens. All of this exploded when it was found out that he had been beating the children for years. This was a secret no longer. His harsh camp experiences could have led to him identifying with the aggressor, a popular psychological mechanism in theories, and doing what he most hated happening to him.

Coincidentally, I recently again met a friend I had worked with in a public assistance center in the South Bronx over thirty years ago. As fate would have it, his son, who owned some South Philadelphia real estate, had the property where the building of the Home for Hebrew Orphans stands in South Philadelphia. He said the building seemed spooky and haunted. Tell me about it!

How much in denial have I been? In the past three years, I have passed the orphanage just down South Third Street hundreds of times on the way to a part-time job and did not know it was there, as I never took the time to really deal with this situation until very recently, when I began writing this book. I never talked to my father about his orphan experiences and wish he were back here now to help me write this book. I guess in a way he is. I dedicate my efforts against corporal punishment to my father in my attempts to break free of denial.

"My policy is not to suppress by force, but to develop by kindness. A bad boy may be kept in check by constant fear of the rod…but it will only suppress, never eradicate, bad behavior." Fleishman (1905) here quotes an unnamed superintendent at the Jewish orphanage in 1888. The officials also in 1888 said that spanking should be a last resort. However, ask my father and Dr Siegel.

MY CAREER

In the beginning of my career I promised myself that I would never work with abused and neglected children. I had seen how New York City child abuse social workers have to make life-or-death decisions. In my job as a public assistance social worker, the great majority of the parents treated their children well and cared about them. Just as with every other social group, there were those who neglected or beat their children; only they had fewer resources to assist them.

When I started with the Philadelphia Department of Public Welfare (DPW), I struggled at first with the issue of parents severely injuring their children, but most of the cases were power struggles and conflicts between parent and child and neglect of all degrees. I wanted to be proactive. I was always fearful that these children would be hurt, and one of my strategies (that I found out quickly was counterproductive) was to tell parents how to stay calm, and if they had to use spanking, to do it with an open hand gently only on the backside. This is unfortunately the technique I still see recommended in many current books of spanking advocates. Fortunately we were supervised closely, and the seasoned supervisors and administrators as well as experienced colleagues in conferences said in no uncertain terms that it was unacceptable to tell parents how to safely spank children. Remember, some of the parents spanked their children and did not leave marks, and some were highly skilled at hitting without physical red marks or bruises. I once had a deaf, emotionally troubled young man whose parents hit him with a pipe with a towel wrapped around it. Denial and craftiness is always a possibility. In society there is much domestic violence, alcohol and drug use, anger, past histories of physical abuse, and rigidity, and there are folks who will say the experts told them spanking is legal and how to do it safely, so it must be okay.

After working at the Camden County Welfare Board, I went to the New School for Social Research in New York City and worked during the day full time, first for the law firm of Lord, Day, and Lord in their library, then as a public assistance caseworker for the New York City Department of Human Services in the South Bronx, where I saw some of the most intense poverty and the pressures of raising children in a dangerous environment. The area I worked in was depicted in the film *Fort Apache: The Bronx*, which showed the decaying conditions of the neighborhoods and the struggles people had to stay safe. When children are raised in a dangerous environment, they can be deeply affected by constantly living under the pressure of daily violence from gangs and people desperate to survive. In many ways it is like growing up in a war zone. Having no laws protecting them from corporal punishment in home compounds the problem. Society puts a green light on a practice that can escalate when parents are under great financial pressure. In any neighborhood, it has been demonstrated that unemployment increases the risk of child maltreatment at home. Children are the weakest and most vulnerable, and too often are lashed out at when the family's finances take a major hit. American laws do not take this into consideration in protecting children.

While in New York, I met my future wife, Vivian, through mutual friends. She was a teacher in Philadelphia, and at the time corporal punishment was legal for children in schools. While she never hit a child, she told me stories of children being paddled by principals. At the time this did not faze me as I had not yet worked with abused and neglected children and had not yet begun to study the

emerging mountain of research on the effect of corporal punishment on children. Again, I had been programmed to assume that
hitting children was fine. It took me years to learn that corporal
punishment of children was a slippery slope. Studying the mountain of research, with my background in psychology, I could understand why so many people sleepwalk through the issue of spanking
and paddling children in home and school. However, that is not
an excuse for me to neglect trying to try to change attitudes on
this practice. In 2002, Pennsylvania made corporal punishment of
children in school illegal due to so many negative experiences and
the assistance of their many medical schools, social work schools,
and universities weighing in on the matter.

For many years, despite years of therapy, I had had great difficulty being comfortable with women because of the difficulties
my mother had with trusting men and the way she had punished
me and my brother with spanking, forcing us to eat soap, shaking,
and ridiculing us. When I finally met the women I would marry, I
treasured this milestone and felt this was my only opportunity, as
Vivian was such a unique, bright, sensitive, and socially conscious
woman.

After nearly twenty-five years of marriage, Vivian developed a soft
tissue swelling behind her knee, which I felt sure was merely like
the temporary swelling she had had in the inner part of her elbow
that turned out to be nothing. However, this new swelling would
not go away, so her primary doctor sent her to an orthopedist, who
x-rayed her and sent her to a world-renowned soft tissue sarcoma
specialist/surgeon in Philadelphia. He found that it was an aggressive cancer. He tried to save her leg, but an operation and radiation
were not successful. He later had to amputate her leg. At first with

high doses of Neuprogen, a rather new treatment drug, the cancer went into remission and then came back. However, even more intense chemotherapy with greater amounts of the drugs sent her cancer into remission. She was on local television in a newscast discussing the miraculous recovery. She learned how to drive with a prosthetic limb after weeks of grueling rehabilitation. She taught school again for a while, and as a little teacher with cancer and a prosthetic limb, never had to resort to corporal punishment in school, as her years of training and firm personality worked, just as it had in tough inner-city neighborhoods in Philadelphia. That is yet another reason I do not believe that corporal punishment in schools is anything but a shortcut that temporarily makes the teachers' jobs easier but comes back to bite them or society later in many cases. After we breathed a sigh of relief, Vivian began having MRIs that showed the cancer was coming back. It spread to her lungs. She died on August 3, 1998.

Two years later, I met my current wife, Dr. Nancy Brown. She proved that I am the luckiest man in the world, as I found love a second time. As a physician, she opposes corporal punishment of children. She has been able to help many of her patients, as she has become skilled at finding abuse in families.

After these experiences, I was searching for a way to protect children in a more preventative way. I wrote three articles published by the National Association of Social Workers on corporal punishment and brain development and how the ethics and values of social workers call for action in confronting the tsunami of denial that this issue seems to bring for so many. I had never written a published article before I retired. I also led workshops with the United Way and the Pennsylvania and Michigan National Association of

Social Workers. In addition, I developed a presentation on public radio, and being on the radio was another first for me.

VOICES IN THE FAMILY

Dr. Dan Gottlieb is an icon in the Philadelphia community who transformed himself, after almost dying in an automobile accident and becoming quadriplegic, into a public radio psychologist (the show's title is above) in Philadelphia and an author. His skills for healing can be sensed when his gentle, comforting voice washes over a pained psyche like an ever-so-slow wave of soothing, warm ocean water. I had the privilege of pitching a show to his director on the effect of child maltreatment on the developing brain that was to include Dr. Paul J. Fink, former president of the American Psychiatric Association. Knowing that I had just retired from the Philadelphia Department of Human Services, there was an effort to rehash old issues on public perception of our agency, but I kept on the topic that was prepared.

Somehow with the advice of a friend in public relations—and this was my first time ever on the airwaves—I was for the most part able to keep the message on the subject. In describing the children's pain and comparing child maltreatment to PTSD, Dr. Gottlieb detected pain in my voice, and he said it seemed from my years working with injured children that I sounded like I had PTSD as well. I had to agree, but I did not discuss the history of my family, which led to this deep sense of angst that I had, though I have discussed it in this book. Nonetheless, Dr. Gottlieb's gentle voice was like a green light, and I had been speaking with the cautionary yellow light on. Corporal punishment has run through my past family life like startling, arousing voices. Gottlieb wrote, "People are hardwired to discriminate, but there is a responsibility to teach a different way."[75] This book tries to take that responsibility.

CHAPTER 6

WHO IS BULLYING WHOM?

Dear Teacher,
I am the survivor of a concentration camp. My eyes saw what no man
should witness. Gas chambers built by learned engineers, children poisoned
by educated physicians, infants killed by trained nurses, and babies shot
and burned by high school graduates. So I am suspicious of education. My
request is that you help your children become more human. Your efforts must
never produce learned monsters, skilled psychopaths, educated Eichmanns.
Reading, writing and arithmetic are only important if they serve to make
our children more human.[76]

This quotation from a Holocaust survivor pleads with educators not to bully or abuse their power, as empathy is the goal, and corporal punishment by teachers violates this sacred responsibility.

How to stop bullying is considered a national priority, but efforts stop short of recognizing that teachers can be bullies. Even in the "helping" professions, bullying can occur by those in the management hierarchy. In her book *Social Workers Bullying: Betrayal of Good Intentions*, Kathrine. Brohl relates that although social workers, psychologists, and psychiatrists are trained to skillfully problem solve, people in management too often abuse their power[77]—if only they could paddle their staff with a rod! Going back to the historic poor law from England's past that is infused in our society, there is an attitude that persons on the lower end of the hierarchy are to blame for societal problems, which is often used as an excuse for the "upper classes" to persecute the poor. One reason Brohl cites is that some managers, as children, were bullies or bullied by other children and along life's journey internalized this behavior to pass down.

Teachers in positions of power, too, may have a tendency to be bullies (Cleaver, 2013).[78] This is not always the case for new teachers, however. For example, new teachers were interviewed in the Mississippi Delta, and key observations were that it pained them to see that corporal punishment and racism were "alive and well" in Mississippi. Most of the white children went to private schools, and there was a continuing segregation-like situation. Since no university supports corporal punishment in school, educators have little knowledge of how to negotiate the culture and legality of child physical punishment in their states.

Some new teachers in Mississippi tried lessons learned in graduate school and persisted in catching the children who were "troublemakers" being good. They found that there often was a payoff for those teachers who were willing to do the hard work of trying different techniques until one worked. A first-year teacher stated that if we try to control children, we are always going to fail. The more gentle approach used by new teachers is similar to what Dr. Herbert Strean (1984) found in mental hospital settings. He cites examples of how new therapists or students in mental hospital settings many times resonated better with schizophrenic patients than the more experienced staff who had been worn down over the years and lost the original spark.[79] The new staff members did not realize that these patients were "hopeless" and treated them in fresh ways.

BULLYING BY TEACHERS IN THE UNITED STATES

Dr. Stuart Twemlow, a psychiatrist who was previously a high school teacher, interviewed 116 teachers, and 45 percent admitted to bullying children; most said it was a hazard of the profession.[80]

My own experiences as a student bear out this high incidence of bullying behavior. When I was in school, it was unfortunately not shocking when Mr. M. threw a chalkboard eraser at a student's head, which missed by an eyelash, or when coaches would openly hit players for not hustling, or when Mr. A. would pick up an attractive high school student in his fancy foreign sports car and brag about it to his students. We have made some progress since then, but not enough to call a teacher a bully and subject him or her to the same rules as bullying students. According to James Garbarino, "The saddest part is that although it is the adults who should be ashamed of bullying children in these ways it is the children who end up feeling ashamed and hurt. It is true that some teachers and adults do not as yet recognize that what they do is bullying, and that is harmful. However, it is both of those things and it needs to stop as *much*, if not more *so*, than student-to-student harassment."[81] Garbarino pinpoints the denial that is so detrimental to children and is another factor in the legal acceptance of corporal punishment in schools. Therefore, despite the strong laws that many states have opposing bullying in school, they still have their blinders about teachers on and walk trance-like into exacerbating the situation.

In his interviews, Garbarino found that for many children, power-abusing teachers are the most frightening aspect of school.

Recently (June 16, 2012), in one of the paddling states, a principal lined up a class of twenty students and encouraged them to hit a grade school student whom he determined was a bully. Who was being the bully?

When my son was eleven, he was bullied by several students. I complained to the school, and nothing was done. Then the bullies bribed a larger child to do the bullying for them, and I brought it up to the school once again. They put me in a room with school personnel and the offending student. I mentioned how this young person needed counseling, and I was berated and ridiculed by the educators for bringing this up in front of the child. I felt bullied by a staff that was not protecting my son.

An incident that further illustrates the denial of teacher bullying occurred when a New Jersey student in a special education class told school administration that a teacher was bullying him, but nobody believed him (Nov.18, 2011). Although it is not legal in New Jersey for a teacher to hit children, this teacher, in a phone-taped moment, shouted the "F-word" at this child and threatened to kick his ass when he was not in the classroom. What would have happened if this teacher had the legal right to use corporal punishment?

There are countless stories of how teachers in states where corporal punishment is permitted by law have taken this bullying to another level. This, again according to research, happens mostly to disabled children, autistic children, and minorities. Yes, bullies often pick on the perceived weakest of children, but then so do teachers who abuse their powers. How do we stop this, or do we need every student to have the incidents taped so people will believe them?

Bullying is such a major problem, and all states set up laws opposed to this behavior by children but not teachers. It seems it is only taken seriously when students videotape the tirades that happen more often than they are acknowledged, frequently against students who are disabled or have ADHD.

Signs a teacher may be bullying a student are, according to Alward:[82]

- complaints of a teacher being *rude,* making sarcastic remarks, or being disrespectful
- complaints of being picked on by a teacher
- complaints of being humiliated by a teacher
- self-deprecating remarks
- headaches, stomachaches, and nightmares that occur frequently
- loss of interest in school
- a resistance to attending school
- negative behavior

WHY DO TEACHERS BULLY?

Teachers are human and have at times frustrating personal lives, addiction, mental illness, and domestic violence in their homes. It is important to be compassionate to teachers, but bullying by teachers can no longer be denied. More importantly, for the best interest of our children, teachers should keep their hands off of paddles and stop striking children as punishment.

In the same study mentioned above, Dr. Twemlow and colleagues (2012)collected information from 116 teachers from seven different schools and found that bullying of students has deep roots in the teachers' early life experiences. Results confirmed that teachers who experienced bullying themselves when young are more likely to both bully students and experience bullying by students both inside the classrooms and outside the classroom. "Factor analysis revealed two types of bullying teacher: a sadistic bully type and a bully victim type." The sadistic type is more in line with those who are insecure and need to pick on weaker individuals.[83]

Another reason that teachers bully is that it is not against the law in many states. The American Supreme Court in 1977 set a precedent that allowed the continuation of legalized bullying in the United States. in the case of *Ingraham versus Wright* centered around a Florida student who was to be paddled in school. He refused. With no court order (it is legal still in Florida to punish students with large wooden paddles), school staff felt that they were safe to force "punishment" upon this student. This principal decided to have a group of teachers hold him down, and he was paddled at least twenty times with a board. He had deep bruising and could not walk for days. This case went to the Supreme Court, and it was ruled that this was not cruel and unusual punishment. This is but one example of the failure of adults in legal precedent decisions to protect children. This permission has been an open invitation, whether the Supreme Court realized it or not, for children to be bullied in schools by too many adults called educators.

THE CONSEQUENCES OF CORPORAL PUNISHMENT IN SCHOOLS

The worst consequence of physical punishment of children is, of course, death. In one infamous case in Japan, a high school basketball coach physically punished a player who subsequently committed suicide. The young man who hanged himself was the captain of the basketball team at Osaka's Sakuranomiya High School. The coach, Ryuji Sonoda, who had physically punished a number of the team members, publicly apologized, but said only that he might or might not have been wrong in using this punishment. The practice was accepted for eighteen years, even though corporal punishment of students is considered a form of bullying in Japan, as Sonada was a successful coach.

In the United States, children have also attempted suicide when physically chastised in school. According to Charlotte Ross, as of 1988, over the past two years, parents and corporal punishment researchers can identify more than two dozen children across the country who have attempted or threatened suicidal behavior after classroom paddling. The following are examples:

[84]J.T., an eight-year-old third-grader, was paddled by an administrator in his school, and his bottom turned purple. He was looking for a gun in his home, as he wanted to kill himself. The family sent him for therapy, and the trained professional concurred that he was severely depressed over the incident. If another child had bullied him into considering suicide, there would have been hell to pay. Teachers, however, have a free pass in many states with wide latitude.

In Dayton, Texas, D.T. had attention deficit disorder and dyslexia, and his parents did not give the school permission to paddle him. He was physically punished anyway, numerous times, for failing to complete homework. The parents had told the teachers that he had learning disabilities and needed special, skillful teaching. D.T.

was too fearful to tell his parents for weeks. He was so distraught that he told his parents he wanted to kill himself and consequently was hospitalized for three months, which cost the parents eighty thousand dollars. This is another Texas horror story. We will deal with Texas again.

In Tennessee, a child, B.A., was recovering from abuse by a baby-sitter and also had learning disorders and hyperactivity. He was paddled almost twenty times by a first-grade teacher. He tried to hang himself.

Why this behavior by teachers is not considered bullying is a mystery. Bullying is a popular cause with everyone now on the bandwagon. Corporal punishment in school is the elephant in the living room that they choose not to see. Politicians rally against bullying by youngsters but do not deal with the adult problem; that is one that they refuse to legislate against.

In 1989, Temple University psychologist, professor, and director of the university's National Center for the Study of Corporal Punishment, Irwin Hyman,[85] researched over two hundred cases of corporal punishment in schools nationwide. He interviewed dozens of children who were so upset by this paddling that they displayed some of the same symptoms of nightmares and depression as combat soldiers. He said he was concerned as a psychologist that the depression and feelings of inadequacy could lead to suicidal thoughts or gestures. Some of the children had to be professionally treated for self-destructive behavior. Hembree stated, "But looking back It is important to remember that Charlotte Ross, head of the Youth National Suicide Center in California, said corporal punishment in school was studied by psychologists over fifteen years, dating back to 1970. They found that physical punishment increases "aggression, vandalism, and juvenile delinquency." Depression and self-destructive behavior also increase.[86]

The devastating effects of corporal punishment have been documented in Korea, as well as in the United States. In South Korea, from 2008 to 2010, suicide has been the leading cause of death for young people. According to E. U. Shin:

> *Corporal punishment is still a popular educational methodology in Korean schools. It is a tradition of Korean education inherited from history. After students receive physical punishment from their teachers, they express their own stress by using violence against other students who are physically weak. Also they react emotionally against the teachers who punished them physically by being irreverent toward them. The teachers, in turn, react emotionally to those students who become disrespectful. In this cycle, emotional conflicts between students and teachers deepen and can become habitual.*

The Koreans found that the lessons of brain science and meditation help the teachers to relax and pry themselves out of the cycle. The students are given alternative behavior methods that include relaxation techniques. Success has been reported in breaking this history of physical punishment leading to more conflict and developing a life of its own. So, although Korea sees the same depression and suicidal ideation as the result of physical punishment that the United States does, the county has set up schools using the latest techniques of behavior management derived from the fruits of the mountain of scientific information from neuroscience.[87]

CORPORAL PUNISHMENT IN TEXAS

Everything in Texas is bigger, including its denial of the effects of physical punishment on children.

A Texas newspaper, the *Dallas News*, recognized the "academic rigor" of Samuel P. Oliner's (2003) research in reviewing his book *Do Unto Others*. The rigorous research, with his findings about corporal punishment of children, is an exercise I wish this Texas newspaper had connected to their state's position on paddling children in school with implements.

This leads to a discussion of Texas as the school corporal punishment capital of the United States. Even Judge William Adams, who rules in a Texas court on child abuse cases, was caught on phone camera by his own daughter, who has cerebral palsy, viciously beating her with a belt and cursing her out as he did so. When this video went viral, he minimized the extent of his behavior, which happens often when men beat wives and, in my experience, when parents beat children.

What did Texas learn from this? Nothing, apparently, as evidenced by a later event in which a male school administrator beat a sixteen-year-old female student's backside with a paddle hard enough to leave purple marks. An outcry arose not only about the paddle but about someone of the opposite sex using such punishment in an area that many consider private. The county snapped into action and passed a ruling that allows educators to paddle members of the opposite sex, as there were not enough female staff to carry out this task on members of their sex.

Texas Governor Rick Perry set up Holocaust panels and organizations in cooperation with his state government. It is unlikely

74

that he knows of the research on lessons of the Holocaust that is opposed to corporal punishment. His schools reflect his lack of understanding of these principles.

Alma Allen, a state representative, has been trying for years to have corporal punishment stopped in Texas schools, with little success. The only glimmer of hope was a regulation that she championed giving parents the right to choose whether a school could paddle their child or not. I spoke to a leading social work educator about the corporal punishment in Texas schools, and he said he thought this had stopped years ago.

In *As Texas Goes,* author G. Collins discusses Texas's fight to block health care for children, among other progressive measures.[88] She also points out that there is no educational training in the University of Texas or any other university in the United States that supports or teaches using physical punishment in schools. In fact, Southern Methodist University in Dallas is one of the most anti corporal punishment schools in the United States. Professor George Holden is one of the top researchers in the world on corporal punishment, and his studies demonstrate the deleterious effects of such physical chastisement. He led a world conference on ending corporal punishment in schools and at home with experts from across the world included. This was in Dallas, Texas.

Dr. Bruce Perry, MD, PhD, is one of the most respected experts in the world on child maltreatment's effect on the brain. He works out of Houston as director of the Child Trauma Academy. He previously was a full professor and head of the neurology department at Baylor University in Waco, Texas. He was a lead researcher and investigator into the David Koresh Waco Cult, where children were abused sexually and physically in a "religiously ritualistic manner." He has written over three hundred journal articles, book chapters, and books. In *Born for Love: Why Empathy Is Essential and Enduring*, he wrote that from the research he did, it followed that spanking and corporal punishment decrease empathy, and this can be a danger to society.[89]

Another prominent Texas researcher who can attest to the dangers of corporal punishment is Dr. Gershoff at University of Texas at Austin. She researched the last thirty years of studies on corporal punishment of children and found that nearly 100 percent of the studies demonstrated the danger of this behavior and/or that it does not improve children's behavior.[90]

CORPORAL PUNISHMENT IN COLORADO

The Holocaust connection moves on. It is ironic that school corporal punishment is still legal in Colorado, as Dr. Henry Kempe, a Holocaust survivor, became a pediatrician and pioneered the field of child abuse and neglect in America in the 1960s.[91] He and Dr. Brandt Steele coined the term *battered child syndrome*, describing how a child may duck and cringe and show other signs of when around the perpetrator or others who may make sudden movements. He was the youngest pediatrician to be department head at the University of Colorado. He spearheaded the efforts to have all fifty states mandate child abuse reporting laws. He also backed the passage of a Colorado bill that deemed abused and neglected children to be entitled to their own legal counsel.

More recently, Colorado has had mass shootings in school and in a theater perpetrated by young people. I would think that a law banning school corporal punishment would be more than welcome in the state, as the research regarding the connection between corporal punishment and aggression backs it. However, for some reason, Colorado, a pioneer in child protection methods and history, as well as home to the American Humane Society, still allows its students to be beaten with wooden and fiberglass paddles and is dropping the ball when it comes to the most positively tested programs in protecting children and consequently the populace of Colorado, for that matter.[92]

The University of Denver and the University of Colorado participated in the Invest in Kids Project, which is a model program. This program seeks to reduce behavior problems and aggressiveness in students in school and home by training children, parents, and teachers. Also, the Incredible Years Program that has proven to be successful in initiating a program to include parents with the children's schooling from zero to twelve years old, using positive discipline, role playing, and brainstorming. Teachers are involved in two training programs in assisting with parental partnering skills, pro-social behavior, and managing the classroom. There is also a training program for teachers to assist children to learn anger management, empathy, and social skills. The programs are named Dina Dinosaur Child Training and Curriculum, respectively.

THE SCOPE OF THE PROBLEM IN AMERICAN SCHOOLS

The White House Conference on Bullying (2011) presented some disturbing information. Thirteen million students, one of three students, are bullied every year. Researchers say these children are at higher risk of getting behind on their studies. Substance abuse, mental health issues, and other health difficulties may occur. Children who are perceived as different because of their poverty, race, sexual orientation, or ADHD or other disability are at greater risk for societal mistreatment according to Maia Szalavitz a prominent author and child advocate[93]

Scherzing School of Welfare California at Berkeley studied over nine hundred parents of children with autism. It was found that 46 percent of these children were bullied, as opposed to 10 percent of non-autistic children. The Sherzing study calls it a public health problem. The fact that teachers in the states where school corporal punishment is legal disproportionately paddle children with autism fits in with the argument that teachers also can be bullies.[94]

Just as teachers' bullying is minimized, so is the bullying that children receive through domestic violence. After years of being largely hidden by society, domestic violence is now considered to be a danger to women and has been the cause of many laws being written. T. D. George discusses how domestic violence negatively affects families for generations.[95] One quarter of all women experience domestic violence in their lifetimes. Children of domestic violence in the home are significantly more likely to receive physical punishments than other children, and even just seeing or hearing the parents abuse each other is often so traumatic that children may have physiological changes that can affect them for life if there is no therapeutic intervention. Denial is often the calling cards of violent families, and some of these children may go to schools where they receive paddling if they demonstrate behavior issues in class.

REASONS ADULTS SHOULD KEEP THEIR CALM

L. Beane gives eight reasons for adults to keep their calm:[96]

1. Children will imitate adults, and the bullying adult serves as a role model to demonstrate that the child's behavior is the way to handle these situations.

2. Physical punishment shows the child that he was right if the adult handles his frustrations in the same manner.

3. Physical punishment may cause a child to temporarily stop that behavior, but this will often lead to new aggressive behaviors.

4. The child will often stop when the punishing adult is around but many times explodes again around another group of people.

5. The young person may displace his anger and physically hit a safer target, or he may just hit the adult who directly beat him.

6. If a child has no fear of authority in the first place, physical punishment may immediately escalate his violence.

7. Relying on punishment may thwart the child's development and saddle him with serious shame and withdrawal.

8. Corporal punishment is only a short-term solution that often fosters copycat behavior in the child.

Furthermore, Beane points out that materials in libraries and bookstores teach how to discipline without the hitting component. There are numerous ways to use relaxation techniques for yourself and the student, and colleagues often have alternate strategies to suggest. He suggests making a pact with a neighboring teacher to temporarily switch classes to allow you to calm down. Even if you are in one of the states that permit corporal punishment of students by law, never spank.

Beane says that teachers are being paid to be the adult and act like one. Even prison guards are not permitted by laws to hit violent prisoners on death row. Teaching is a profession, and to be a professional, one must study the latest research and techniques on the subject. If a teacher shirks his responsibility and stoops to hit a child, he is ignoring almost three decades of research on the dangers of physical punishment on the developing child's brain.

Thank goodness teachers are cannot be physically punished for failing to do their homework on classroom management!

CHAPTER 7

SCIENCE BE DAMNED

The Nazis' approach to science was twisted and frequently denied the truth to form persecutory arguments against the Jews. Dr Mengele performed horrid research involving torturing and killing Jewish children and twins. The Jewish children were used as guinea pigs, and their parents were exterminating using science to justify this travesty. To deny the research on child corporal punishment is a different way of twisting the lessons of scientists.

HOW PHYSICAL PUNISHMENT AFFECTS THE BRAIN

"Neuroscience describes spanking as a brain bath, or in other words it's like being under water at a pool; you can hear people talking but you cannot understand what they are saying," according to Robbyn Peters-Bennett.[97] Cortisol and adrenaline are released during a spanking, and the ability to learn and recognize the meaning of what transpired is blocked by a physiological freezing, where the child learns to be on guard and "hyper-vigilant."

In my opinion, not since the wave of radiology ushered in a more scientific study of child abuse and neglect has a scientific wave been so enlightening. Neuroscience is demonstrating in terms of brain structures, hormones, and physiology the detrimental effect child maltreatment has from childhood to the last breath a person takes.

Neuroscience tells us first of all that the human brain has its own radar that scans the environment for danger from the earliest days of infancy. The part of the brain that does the scanning is the amygdala, a walnut-shaped structure on both sides of the limbic system in the midbrain region. The lower part of the brain is the oldest, and the brain stem controls breathing, heart rate, neglect, or other maltreatment. The amygdala's messages of danger and fear are not carried to the frontal lobe of the brain to be processed but go to the lower brain to protect us in a flight or fight mode. Neuroscience also shows that if treated early, the brain has plasticity, which can compensate.

The frontal cortex region is the reasoning sector, and with too much stress the messages never reach this upper level, so panic or freezing can be the response based on body warning signals from the lower brain, but travel directly to the midbrain's amygdala and lower brain stem.

I believe hitting a child is often a sign of parental loss of control, a reaction that doesn't require any thought. In fact, it is a way of stopping the child's thoughts as well as actions, as I can attest from my own experience of being on the receiving end of physical punishment; my battle of wills with my father did not increase our understanding of each other. "The entire transaction is stuck at the behavioral level, triggering powerful sub-cortical emotions of rage, resentment, and fear—the activated amygdala—without involving a process of reflection."[98]

Certainly this quote from Dr. Susan Gerhardt matches the experiences I had as a child and captures points that I wish to convey in this chapter. The fact that reflection is a victim of the corporal punishment process affects paddled schoolchildren as well. Empathy is also a victim here, which is the building block to successful give-and-take relationships, and, if missing in action, decreases the possibility of peace on a multitude of levels. Gerhardt further states, "Although we have been able to invest in expensive experimental research into early psychological and brain development—research has consolidated the insights of attachment theory—we are not making use of this knowledge" of the body.[99]

HOW PHYSICAL PUNISHMENT AFFECTS BEHAVIOR

Brain World (spring 2010, p. 56–57), a major news magazine published over the past few years by the International Brain Education Association, has an article in a special section called "Beliefs and Values That Changed in Education since 1965."[100] The article has a grid with the latest accomplishments in the educational sphere that have relationships to research on the brain. In Figure 5.1, under "Beliefs and Values," the old view listed is "Children would learn best from being spanked or paddled. Corporal punishment was the best way to teach children proper behavior. Fear of being paddled would prevent disruptive actions." The old method under the heading "Practice" states, "If students' behavior disrupted the class, or if disrespect was shown towards adults, paddling would be instituted. A teacher's refusal to paddle children would be referred to the principal."

Under the "enlightened" improvements since 1965, with the heading "Change," the article states unconditionally that "school physical punishment was banned" (unfortunately, too good to be true).

It states under the "Learning Issues" heading that you should not be forced to do something morally wrong, "even if it meant there was a chance to lose one's position." If only this were true! This gives the false impression that there are not nineteen US states where punishing children with paddles is legal. Perhaps assumptions like this are a reason the majority of professionals and the public in general that I speak to is stunned when they learn that children are still lawfully being beaten in schools. This is an example of the need for an accurate public relations campaign for the safety of our children against legalized child abuse.

Dr. Martin E.B. Seligman, former president of the American Psychological Association and renowned professor at the University of Pennsylvania for decades, is considered an expert in the scientific study of what effective, evidence-based psychological therapy and research entail. He describes Dr. Alan Kazdin as representing the "gold standard" for understanding the methods for parents to deal with challenging child behavior.[101] Kazdin writes, "But let me underscore that science doesn't show any value at all in hitting children, and does show that physical punishment, even when moderate and not abusive, can have long term negative consequences for physical health (it's associated with more illnesses, earlier than usual death in adulthood), mental health (higher rates of psychiatric disorders in adulthood), and academic problems (children do more poorly in school and drop out of high school at higher rates). And yet research on the United States shows that everyday methods of punishment still include spanking for most children."[102] Without any question, this is the closest to unanimous researchers are in coming to a conclusion. Elizabeth Gershoff's review of the last thirty years of research confirms this fact.[103]

There is an argument that the research, although voluminous, in favor of not using corporal punishment of children must be 100 percent flawless to be accepted. Research does not have to be done over and over again nor expected to be flawless for others, such as adult women, to have legal protection against physical chastisement. A different and nearly impossibly high standard is demanded to demonstrate that corporal punishment of children, including slapping and spanking, is harmful. The meager amount of research claiming that it is acceptable to use corporal punishment on children is magnified and embraced by social and religious conservatives.

Kazdin says that physical punishment should include a warning label for side effects similar to prescription medicine.[104] Here are some of the side effects that he notes:

1. Recovery from punishment—Again, the most critical point is that punishment usually does not have the enduring effect of reducing and eliminating behavior. But sometimes it has a very different enduring effect, one that's bad for both child and parent. "What happens is that the child adapts to the punishment; the technical term for this is recovery from punishment." This often leads to escalating punishment to try to stop the behavior, and the child may still continue to have the recovery effect, which spirals out of control. Unfortunately the parent may hit harder and use a belt.

2. Emotional reactions—At first the child may seem upset and cry or scream, giving a false positive indication that the punishment is working.

3.   Escape and avoidance—The child may avoid parents or teachers and not come to them when he needs help.

4.   Aggression—Numerous studies demonstrate that physical punishment can lead to escalating retaliation that may include fighting back, sabotage, and bullying.

5.   Modeling punishment—As Bandura's studies show, children imitate their parents and sometimes will hit dolls and other children.[105] It is known from research that children "discipline their peers in the same ways parents discipline them."

PHYSICIANS' VIEWS ON CORPORAL PUNISHMENT

According to T. Berry Brazelton only in the last few decades have pediatric physicians begun studying child development as a major portion of their training.[106] They *had* studied the pathology and disease, and he and a group of colleagues toiled to change this situation by developing professional societies that studied the developmental approach. A study in 1968 found that 70 percent of family physicians supported spanking, and 59 percent of pediatricians also endorsed corporal punishment, usually in the form of spanking. With the greater emphasis on developmental research over the past decade, the American Academy of Pediatrics has recommended against spanking both at home and in schools. So the learning curve has been slow despite the fact the numerous European and other countries have established legal bans on spanking in school and at home.

Therefore, even for professionals the change has been slow but is now rapid and steady. It is easy to see why the public has been slow

86

to be aware of and understand the four decades of research that is overwhelmingly finding the dangers of such punishment when pediatricians' advice is ignored on a massive scale.

In 2013, Brent and Silverstein discussed the ominous implications of childhood adversity and child maltreatment.[107] "Physicians must also be advocates for social policies that can help achieve what all parents want—a secure environment for their children to develop into competent adults as mentioned." This also includes trying to advocate for policies to end child poverty, according to Brent and Silverstein.

The American Academy of Pediatrics is opposed to school corporal punishment based on decades of research and clinical experience. Yet two physicians (not pediatricians and not as knowledgeable about children as those specialists) refused to vote for a bill to end corporal punishment in all states.

THE SEXUAL SIDE OF CORPORAL PUNISHMENT

The concern about the sexual side effects of corporal punishment is long-standing.

George Scott, in *The History of Corporal Punishment*, vehemently states, "It would have been easy to ignore the sexual side and all its implications, as so many writers on the subject of corporal punishment have done before. But this ostrich-like attitude would have not only to evade, but to present distortion of the truth and this one ground alone ranks as a form of punishment out of tune with modern scientific reformative and educational trends."[108] He further states, "Every sexologist knows that the number of individuals who have experienced sexual feelings while being whipped is a considerable one, and in nearly every instance where the anomaly has persisted in adult life the victim is able to trace the beginning of his perverse interest in flagellation to a flogging received at school or elsewhere."[109]

The issue of child sexual abuse is gaining rapid consensus of its destructive nature. However, it has only been taken seriously as a problem for about thirty years, as evidenced by the large number of relatively recent cases of clergy being held accountable for their actions. Although many experts point out scientifically that spanking can cause damage to nerves and cause great problems concerning sexuality, denial still reigns supreme.

The word *spank* has several connotations; as we discussed, the act occurs on an erogenous area. The word *spank* is linked with the novel *Fifty Shades of Grey* in a parody that was not sanctioned by the author, E. L. James. The plot of this parody involves a man trying to make his girlfriend submissive in many sadomasochistic ways. The title of this play is *Spank!: The Fifty Shades Parody*. As researcher R. J. Stoller writes, there is a potential connection between pain and sexuality in spanking,[110] and this is not lost on this play. Dr. Haim Ginott (1961) discussed this in his book over forty years ago.

There also are questions about adult males paddling/spanking children and female teenage students in schools. A case was recently examined in Texas by J. and D. O. Friel, who concur that not until the last thirty years has sexual abuse of children been seen as a serious problem.[111] In a 1967 comprehensive textbook of psychiatry, esteemed psychiatrists Kaplan and Freedman write in a chapter that incest was a rare (one out of a million) behavior.[112]

They also said that the psychological harm of child sexual abuse was inconclusive in the research. In fact, from *Freud's* days until the 1970s, child sexual abuse was not labeled as a major problem.

HOW CORPORAL PUNISHMENT WORSENS ADVERSE CHILDHOODS

Attachment Parenting is a large-scale organization devoted to informing the public about the latest well-researched child-rearing methods that are available and ready to assist in the difficult task of being a parent. One of their leaders, Rita Brehl, states in *Psych Central*:

> *Seemingly more so than any other part of society, childrearing is slow to catch up with what research shows are the best practices. The medical community, the automotive industry, even lawn chemicals seem to advance more quickly in finding what is healthiest for families and communicating it to parents. We don't see parents treat strep throat with hydrogen peroxide any more they go to the doctor for a prescription of antibiotics. We know that children are safest in the back seat of the car and which car seat works best for each age group. And in the case of lawn chemicals, we know that when dad is spraying the yard, to keep the kids in the house. But there are still so many pervasive myths alive today regarding child rearing.[113]*

One logjam on the professional level, according to McCall and Groark, is that researchers generally do not disseminate their findings to the "three Ps, the public, policy makers, and the practioners."[114]

Several researchers have written about the need to use discipline other than corporal punishment with attachment-disordered children.[115] They recommend caretakers use other limiting discipline rather than spanking these children: "...Caretakers of these wounded children must develop their capacity to provide empathy and attunement, reflective sensitive experiences with the child." Handling attachment trauma from a traumatic childhood requires skill and patience. Unfortunately, American adoptive parents have often been unable to properly deal with attachment problems in international children adopted, and the consequences too often have been regrettable and dangerous to the children.

Domestic violence is another factor that compounds the problems of corporal punishment. According to the Domestic Violence Resource Center, 75 percent of all US citizens know a family member or someone who is a victim of domestic violence.[116] Thirty percent know someone who was abused by a spouse or partner within the last year. It was also found that 50 percent of children in homes with domestic violence are also physically punished or assaulted. Why would pro-spankers in any way give permission for parents to spank or use corporal punishment knowing that a good portion of their audience are victims of domestic violence and the perpetrators most likely are not rational in their use of physical force?

These figures do not account for all the parental alcohol and drug abuse, mental illness, and unresolved anger issues. Add in the denial that is often a part of these conditions, and one could say pro-spankers are lighting a fuse on the potential for violence toward children.

Anger is not the only issue involved in domestic violence. According to recent figures (2011), 40 percent of forty-six depressed dads who were studied spanked their children, as opposed to 13 percent of dads who were not depressed.[117] Also, these dads spent less time reading to their children and bonding with them (Estimates are that fifteen million children are living with a depressed parent, although it is probably more).

A massive study that Felitti, Anda, and other researchers conducted over the course of more than two decades with nearly twenty thousand patients in the Kaiser Health System studied the effect of adverse childhoods.[118] Many of these childhoods included the physical and/or sexual abuse, drugs and/or alcoholism in the family, incarceration of parents, domestic violence, loss (such as abandonment or death of the parent), and mental illness of one or both of the parents. The researchers found that the more of each of these adverse childhood experiences a person had, the greater the probability was that he or she would have concrete serious emotional and physical conditions in later life. Some of the conditions were serious mental illness and heart and lung problems, which affect the quality and length of life. These studies were repeated over many years in massive numbers. A reputable ally in these studies was the Center for Disease Control under the research of Dr. Robert Anda. The CDC developed a questionnaire for people to fill out to chart how they fared on these adverse childhood factors.

These factors are brought into school by many of the children with the most troubles coping with school. Also a number of teachers undoubtedly had such childhoods, with a varying number of adverse effects. I suggest that the children most likely to be paddled in school are the same ones who have the most adverse variables and cards stacked against them.

In *Classroom Management That Works: Research-Based Strategies for Every Teacher* by R. J. Marzano, J. S. Marzano, and D. J. Pickering, the review of the research data suggests that there are many underlying causes why students are problematic and misbehave in school.[119] This dovetails with the factors in the ACE studies conducted by Felitti. "These students enter the classroom with a staggering array of serious issues in their lives." Thompson and Wyatt report that a large number of students in school referred for behavioral problems have a history of physical and sexual abuse in their lives; this has been reported to be as high as "60 to 70 percent" of these referred students.[120]

Marzano and Pickering (2003) state that millions of Americans are homeless each year, and 40 percent of these people have children. Twenty percent of children are raised in families that have alcohol problems. One and a half million students have an incarcerated parent; 15.7 million students live in poverty with their families; 5 percent of children between nine and seventeen are depressed, and only a small number are actually treated.

Seven percent of children have ADHD, and most of those have it combined with other conditions. These include anxiety disorders, mood disorders, and learning difficulties, to name a few. The contributions of science have been largely ignored in those nineteen states where paddling is still legal in school.

In ten- to fourteen-year-olds, suicide is the fourth leading cause of death in the United States. Add to this that the children most likely to be paddled are black males and students with ADHD or other disabilities and we have a clear civil rights violation occurring. The children with the most obstacles to face are overrepresented in the children who receive this "legalized abuse" from educators.

In *High Price,* Dr. Carl Hart (2013), neurology professor at Columbia University, discusses support systems and how they can overcome the negative effects of corporal punishment as well as drug habits. He states that research shows that minority children receive a disproportionate amount of physical punishment in schools. Parents often feel that males need to be careful not to attract negative attention, as they are more likely to be chastised at school and by police. Therefore, many parents use corporal punishment because they believe it will keep the child afraid of authorities and in that manner protect him. This punishment can backfire, according to Hart; he says only extended family members protected him from being a part of this pattern. Police would come often during episodes of domestic violence in his home but always let his father off the hook. He studies the patterns of discrimination that make black males more likely to be arrested and become part of the punitive system.

The National Health and Safety Performance Standards: Guideline for Out-of-Home Care Programs is endorsed by the American Academy of Pediatrics, American Public Health Association, and US Department of Health and Human Services Division of Health Services and Services Administration, Maternal and Child Health Bureau.[121] This manual lists prohibited behaviors (for all children in out-of-home programs and caretakers), including "corporal punishment including beating, spanking, shaking, and pinching..." The rationale is that "research links corporal punishment with negative effects such as later criminal behavior and impairment of learning," and "corporal punishment may be physical abuse or may easily become physical abuse." Aside from these agencies, the American Medical Association, the American Psychological Association, the National Association of Social Workers, the

American Bar Association, and too many others to mention are opposed to corporal punishment in schools. In fact, over one hundred organizations that I contacted recommend against corporal punishment in out-of-home settings.

Is a school not an out-of-home setting? The question is why do nineteen states continue to allow corporal punishment by law? Many children are severely beaten, and this is masked by widespread efforts to protect the educators who perpetrate these actions from legal liability. As mentioned, overrepresented students who receive this punishment are the disabled and black students. There is a civil rights aspect to this problem.

There is a children's rights issue as the only people in the United States who may be paddled/spanked by those who care for them, including prisoners on death row. Soldiers in the military may not legally be physically punished. How did we reach this irrational, dangerous treatment of our children?

EMPATHY AND AGGRESSION

In his so-called Bobo experiments, Albert Bandura found that children who witness the experience of an inflatable clown being hit are more likely to use such methods when in play situations themselves.[122] This is backed up by the research on the effects of corporal punishment that found that children from three to five are more aggressive when spanking is used. Researchers in neurobiology have also found mirror neurons in the brain that facilitate the imitating of behavior experienced. Again, if a child is hit or sees an example of this behavior, he is much more likely to imitate it. I have seen countless times when children hit their dolls in imitation of what they experienced in their home environments.

Research shows that children in homes where there is domestic violence are more likely to take on those roles later. More children in these homes are likely to be physically hit for punishment. Why don't we connect the dots between all the factors in generational behavior taught and handed down to receptive minds?

Prolific researcher Bruce Perry, one of the world's top experts on the effect of child maltreatment on the developing brain, affirms that spanking is not conducive to empathy. He states, "Needless to say spanking is or any other form of harsh discipline does not and cannot encourage empathy."[123] (He says "needless to say," but it needs to be said.) "To encourage empathy, discipline by reasoning, perspective taking, consistency of appropriate consequences, and above all love. Research shows that children who receive corporal punishment are more aggressive, more likely to be antisocial as teenagers, and even have lower IQs than those who are not physically disciplined."

On the positive side, if a child experiences skillful parenting with the warmth and role modeling necessary, he or she is more likely to develop empathy. This is just one of countless reasons that a positive approach to discipline is better for the child and the future of society in general. Why is this not counted by perhaps a majority of parents in with all the reasons not to hit children? An eminent researcher in this field of neurobiology, Marco Iacoboni, sees three factors why denial of scientific research in this area is so rampant[124]. First, in the realm of policy making, science is "confined to the ivory tower." Iacoboni would like to see this information on mirroring and imitation inform policy making. What one learns as a child and believes is hard to change, and spanking certainly has been prominent in the vast majority of homes as modeling how to raise children.

Iacoboni also notes that children with autism imitate the action of a person without a solid understanding of the meaning behind the imitation. Therefore, if a child is spanked, he or she may learn how to hit but not why the person is acting this way.

D. D. Simons and S. K. Wurtele further found that parents who spank children are more likely to have children who believe in and act on using physical hitting to solve their problems with other children[125]. This supports research on bullies being more likely to have received corporal punishment as children. The authors conclude that practitioners should encourage parents to avoid corporal punishment as a disciplinary method, which could lead to a change in attitudes and behaviors of the next generation of parents to mitigate brutal practices. But wait...please read the next paragraph.

MOST AMERICANS OPPOSED TO CORPORAL PUNISHMENT IN SCHOOL

An ABC poll conducted in November 2012 found that "even in the South...just 35 percent think spanking should be allowed in schools."[126] In the rest of the country the number supporting spanking in school is 26 percent. Not only does an avalanche of research over decades demonstrate the danger of school corporal punishment, but the public, even in those regions where corporal punishment is legal, does not seem to want this type of school/government authority in punishing children. Rationally it appears that there should be no question that it be outlawed in every state in the United States. Two things that might keep it going are the generations of corporal punishment that have imbedded it in the fabric of our American child-rearing practices and the fact that some people of faith believe in the original sin that is said to be ingrained in infants and must be corrected.

According to polls, in educated groups there is much less physical punishment of children than in less educated groups. What does that tell you about who believes in beating schoolchildren, and then why do these educated educators use this physical punishment on children? Has the lower part of their brains taken over, or are they afraid of being fired for not following rules? This again gets into the tendency of people to do as authority figures say, as Stanley Milgram documented in his experiments (discussed at the end of chapter 1).

Even in many of the states where corporal punishment is allowed, authorities recognize the danger and potential liability of physically punishing children in school.[127] They have therefore instituted "safeguards" such as limiting the number of swats allowed, requiring witnesses, making sure corporal punishment is a last resort, and, in some districts, ensuring that the person spanking is not the one making the complaint to assure emotions do not get involved. They also recommend that the size and health of the children to be struck must be carefully accounted for in this subjective set of rules that changes from state to state and district to district. Different states and districts have different requirements for the instruments to be used for the thrashing. Some states take parents' wishes into account, and some do not. Do we need federal government standards for a science of failsafe physical punishment in schools?

What are we doing to our children? Either there is great denial or lack of caring about the safety of children. If adults in positions of authority cannot harness the frontal lobes of their brains to make rational decisions, how do we expect the children whose brains have not fully developed in the frontal lobes to act and not learn violence from being struck with paddles in school? As many parents say, if we are not allowed to hit children with large wooden paddles, how come teachers do and are protected by law most times even when they grossly get out of control themselves?

CHAPTER 8

SPORTS AND WRESTLING WITH "CORPORAL PUNISHMENT"

You can't make this up. Daniel Dean McDevitt is a professional wrestler known as "Corporal Punishment," and we will see that he is far from the only corporal punishment in sports. In Hudson, Florida, another former wrestler, Dean Liptak, now a teacher, wrote a question for his math students: "A fifty kg student has a momentum of 500 kg *mjs* as the teacher launches him near a wall. What is the velocity of the student heading toward the wall?" He also had a question about the velocity of a speeding car moving toward running over a baby. He is in Florida, where corporal punishment is legal in schools. His math questions caused an outcry from parents.

If you think this was an isolated incident, consider that in Gwinnett County, Georgia, at Beaver Ridge Elementary School, third-graders were given these math questions by teachers: "If Frederick got two beatings per *day*, how many would he get in two weeks?" and "Each tree had 56 oranges. If 8 slaves pick them equally, *then* how much would each slave pick?"[128] This led to a vehement outcry from many parents that reached the major news networks. The school district's spokesperson stated, "In this one the teachers were trying to do a cross curricular activity." The reason for this, she said, was to mesh social studies with math problems. This is how ingrained these attitudes toward corporal punishment are, and the people making the laws do little to change these attitudes toward treatment of children, mostly black males and disabled children, by turning their backs on school paddling.

Delving more into attitudes in schools toward child abuse, long before the Penn State scandal, the sports world had a long history of coaches maltreating children and youths. In fact, in Brook deLench's 2006 book, *Home Team Advantage*, she calls on moms to monitor coaches' contact with their children at all levels of education as physical, emotional, and sexual abuse has been all too *common,* with parents and children often being overly trusting.[129] She cites Dr. Eli Newberger, pediatrician from Harvard Medical School, as saying that besides moms and dads, pediatricians, teachers, principals, and coaches should be required to read that book. deLench recommended that HR Bill 5628 be passed by Congress to stop legalized child abuse, corporal punishment, in schools. Nobody listened.

As I am writing this book, my alma mater, Rutgers, is providing an example of coaches bullying students as Mike Rice, basketball coach, pushed his players, threw basketballs at them, and relentlessly cursed at them. This behavior was captured on phone cameras. Rutgers administration was in hot water, as several months after viewing these tapes they did nothing. This led to the coach and athletic director being fired and negative national publicity. Just when I thought Rutgers was moving in a mature manner by firing Mike Rice and the athletic director, they hired Judith Herman, and it was later found out that she had been relieved of her duties as volleyball coach at the University of Tennessee for calling her female players countless profanities and adding that they were "whores."

In Chicago, high school sports programs were plagued with coaches beating players. Arne Duncan, then superintendent of Chicago schools, later secretary of education, vehemently denounced corporal punishment in schools and sports. He promised to end this problem in no uncertain terms. However, when he became the US Secretary of Education, he wilted and said it is up to the individual states if corporal punishment should occur in their schools.

Now (violent) American football has inadvertently given the media evidence against child corporal punishment and maltreatment by presenting outrageous situations that must be resolved. In Pulaski, Arkansas, a football player at a reunion cried after recalling being beaten with a paddle in school. In Dallas, a coach hit a football player with a large wooden paddle that broke during the beating and was re-taped so the beating could continue. The coach said he was just trying to help the player "make it in life."

At the college level, Mike Mangino was leading a successful Kansas University program that he had built. Then he was caught poking players in the chest and using derogatory epithets. In April 2013, an article in the *New York Times* entitled "A Sad History of Abusive Coaches," documented how Mangino and a Texas Tech football coach were fired for brutal practices that were at one time condoned.[130] This included pushing and slapping.

Thirty years ago, educators assigned a six-foot-three, 210-pound high school football player, Dick Schafrath, the task of punishing children who were acting poorly in his school. He frequently did this with wooden paddles. This experience so traumatized him that after an all-pro football career as a Cleveland Browns lineman in the most violent of sports, he turned his pain into compassion for children. As a Republican state senator for over twenty years, he introduced several bills to outlaw physical punishment in school, and just in 2009 it was passed. Governor Strickland, a Democrat who was a prison psychologist (and saw many examples of abused children in that population), signed the bill to overturn this barbaric practice.

CHANGES IN THE CULTURE OF CORPORAL PUNISHMENT

Can sports be a forum to lessen the incidents of physical punishment? In Croatia, the answer may be yes. There a current national football team (okay, it's soccer) has banded together to protest corporal punishment of children. What about in the United States? There are hopeful signs there, as well. In his book *How Football Explains America*, Sal Paolantonio examines how current coaches have reflected the culture of paternal authority and corporal punishment., , but as the culture changes football coaches and other sport leaders are beginning to reflect the new way America is beginning to approach corporal punishment of youth..[131] Once upon a time, there were burly football players in their teens who were being paddled (a long-standing practice) by the coaches, and the football gods said, "Thou shall not hit these large warriors as they are vulnerable and at great risk." How did this change come to be, and what can it mean for our society? de Lench (2008) rallies mothers to protect their young from any physical chastisement in *Home Team Advantage: The Critical Role of Mothers in Team Sports*. Hopefully this will be a barometer of future change.[132]

Hannah Storm, sports anchor at ESPN, weighs in on the subject of corporal punishment in sports by coaches and other adults in *Go Girl! Raising, Healthy, Confident, and Successful Girls through Sports*. She writes, "Coaches who use physical contact as punishment are guilty of abuse...even if this happens just once it is imperative that you report the incident to the program administrators so they can sanction the coach."[133] Brook de Lench (2006) echoes the same message in her book. She says to talk with the coach, and if not satisfied, go to higher authorities.

When I read all-pro legendary basketball player Jerry West's 2011 book, even as an adult, I was jealous of his chutzpah in confronting his father about the fact that he received physical punishment from his dad, and he stated how he was angry his whole life.[134] He did not appreciate his own achievements, as he felt he was that little boy who had to be perfect and nothing he did was good enough. My low chutzpah did not allow me to discuss the painful past much with my parents. This book appears to have been cathartic for the jump shooter, whose silhouette is used for the iconic National Basketball League symbol on millions of basketball items, including the jersey my brother just purchased for me.

The Philadelphia Phillies began a pilot program to train their staff how to work with children and adults with autism who go to the ballgames. It requires training, sensitivity, and respect to treat citizens on the autism spectrum in a manner that respects their rights and dignity. Efforts are being made to sensitize the day-of-game staff to understand that people with autism can be overwhelmed by sensory stimulation. Often they cannot look into people's eyes as they interact. Out of frustration they can have some tantrums, as variance from routine can be painful for them. The ballpark and the crowds can be disorienting to them. Therefore a group of experts is presenting Phillies' staff with a series of discussions, step by step, about behavior at a sporting event. For example, people with autism are often out of sync with their environments and social interactions when touch is involved. A *touch* that could be considered comforting to most people could set off defensive behavior and overwhelm these individuals. If only this message spurred changes in laws to protect children with autism from corporal punishment. After all, in other issues, these children are receiving growing support.

While the New York Mets are often a hated rival for Philadelphia Phillies fans such as myself, I must reluctantly give them credit for their sensitivity to the needs of children with autism. After taking the 7 subway train to Citi Field, I was surprised that the public address speaker system was so low in the ballpark. At first I attributed it to the fact that our seats were in the third-level stratosphere. However, I was pleasantly surprised that on this Autism Awareness Day, the volume was turned down, which would protect the fans with autism from overstimulation. Also, the music was unusually soothing for a ballgame, again for the comfort of these fans. I thought, *If only the nineteen states that allow for legally hitting children (and a disproportionate number of students with autism) would learn from professional baseball instead of taking the shortcut in swatting these children when they misbehave or are many times misunderstood.*

Major League Baseball may have a growth hormone problem, but it is light-years ahead of the US states that blatantly trample the rights of these children.

Let's make it a strikeout for corporal punishment of children instead of striking out at the children.

CHAPTER 9

A HISTORY OF CHILD MALTREATMENT

Maltreated children have historically been used for property, profit, sexual gratification, displacing frustrations of everyday life, and as scapegoats and vehicles to literally beat forces such as Satan out of them.

Many children were seen as burdens. In ancient societies such as the Roman Empire, infanticide was all too common. Children who were considered weak or ill could be and often were killed or severely injured, mostly by the rule of their fathers.

Margaret Mead discussed a widespread taboo in almost all groups against incest.[135] Nonetheless, in all societies, countless stories of incest abound.

Child labor has been rampant throughout the world. In many countries, child labor exists to this day, accounting for some of our favorite athletic shoes and designer clothes.

Until fifty years ago, there were literally no definitions, criteria, or laws to protect children from abuse. In the United States, there has been a proliferation of laws largely formed, interpreted, and carried out by individual states. This leaves essentially dozens of different definitions of child abuse and neglect, which do not appear to have as a common denominator the best interests of the child based on medical, psychological, and clinical science and experience. This can be seen in the incredibly varied degrees to which some states set hodgepodge laws to allow children to be paddled in schools or to ignore the issue and even protect educators who punish children with beatings from liability, even if such corrective measures go way overboard.

Another historical view of childhood will hopefully be studied. According to E. Young-Bruehl, in her 2012 book, *Childism*, we need to study how children have been denied rights since the earliest times.[136] She notes, "Since the mid twentieth century, social scientists have been exploring the many reasons why adults harm individual children but they have not looked at the wider picture of how harm to children is rationalized and normalized." K. B. Walant wrote "normative abuse shifts with societal customs and traditions. What we would consider today physical abuse was viewed as normative one hundred years ago, and was not then considered abuse."[137] This likely pertains to child corporal punishment/spanking. But perhaps the future can be a nearer future. Although the treatment of children has improved on some levels, they still do not vote, and they are largely invisible when it comes to granting them rights. It takes a long time to change conceptions of abuse even when the standards are understood.

THE FOUNDING FATHERS' VIEWS ON CORPORAL PUNISHMENT

"The rights of minors are as sacred as the rights of the aged", said Thomas Paine, one of America's founding fathers.[138] Paine valued children's rights more than our current leaders do. Another founding father, Dr. Benjamin Rush, was a champion for children and advocated loudly and sensitively that children away from home, in schools or institutions, should not receive physical punishment. The current politicians trumpet our forefathers but there's not a sound to stop corporal punishment of our children. The "We, the people" refrain includes children!

Our founding fathers were a theme of President Obama's 2013 inauguration speech supporting more equal treatment for American citizens. Our forefathers are also referred to by Tea Party Republicans when it comes to gun rights, individual rights, and taxation rights. One never hears a politician mention the founding father of psychiatry Benjamin Rush's position on children's rights, as children cannot vote. He was the founder of the first United States hospital, and he was a devout Christian who believed in most of the ideals of conservatives.[139] Benjamin Rush founded the first Bible society in America. He stated in a devout manner, "The Bible, when not read in schools, is seldom read in any subsequent period in life...The Bible...should be read in schools in preference to other books because it contains the greatest portion of that kind of knowledge which is calculated to produce private and public happiness." Within that framework, he was vehemently opposed to school and institutional corporal punishment. He wrote about his strong opinions in this regard.[140]

Following in Rush's footsteps, every recognized medical and child's advocacy group is vehemently opposed to physical punishment of children in schools. This includes the American Medical Association, American Academy of Pediatrics, and the American Bar Association. The medical industry, dating back to its American roots, therefore has been opposed to children being beaten, usually with wooden or fiberglass paddles in school.

CURRENT ACTION AND INACTION REGARDING CORPORAL PUNISHMENT

Fast-forward to 2010 and 2011, when Bills 5628 and 3027 were presented to the Congressional Education and Workforce Committee proposing to stop the legalized child abuse that is corporal punishment in nineteen states where it is still accepted by law. Each bill died from lack of congressional support. Two physicians on the committee, both from Tennessee , failed to support these bills despite the fact that every credible medical group in the United States, including the American Medical Association and American Academy of Pediatrics, vehemently opposed this practice based on the three decades of research demonstrating the dangers. These two are Dr. David "Phil" Roe and Dr. Scott Desjarlais, respectively. One of those physicians is Methodist, and that church strongly approved two policies denouncing corporal punishment in schools as dangerous and said that Jesus would not condone such a practice. The Methodist church recommended that all church members contact their governmental representatives to make this practice illegal. I spoke to a member of the child advocacy branch of the Methodist church, who expressed regret that the thirty years of research on the subject was neglected. It was a courageous move for the Methodist church to adopt these policies, since their founder, John Wesley, advocated physically punishing children, including babies, to break the evil nature that was liter-ally interpreted as a manifestation of the devil. The chair of the committee, John Kline, who has the power to move the bill to be reviewed by the committee or put up a block, is also a practic-ing Methodist who bucked his own religion's principals by voting against this measure.

The first surgeon general, Benjamin Rush, was, as stated, vehe-mently opposed to physical punishment of children in school. Ronald Reagan's surgeon general, C. Everett Koop, one of the foremost children's surgeons who ever lived, shared this disdain for school corporal punishment:

> *I've read all the stories in the newspapers and weekly magazines about the principals who have cleaned up their schools by physical force. And I am ashamed for them, for their communities, and for any of my fellow Americans who think such principals have the "right idea." They do not. There was never a time when a major social problem was solved by beating a child and there will never be such a time...For centuries adults have injured children and lied about it, and other adults have heard those lies and then merely turned away...Instead of that, we must be putting the blame where it belongs: perhaps on some other human being, most likely an adult, who did the wrong thing intentionally or unintentionally, but not accidentally...C.E.Koop, Keynote Address to the Children's Symposium(Washington,D.C. Uniting America to Fight Childhood, Injury,1989)*

In the book *Presidents Helping Children*, M. Petit discusses what presidents have done to improve the rights of children.[141] While no president has directly entered a position on legally stopping corporal punishment of children in school or home, they have over the years made progress in other areas, often against steep odds imposed by their colleagues in the House of Representatives and Senate. Every Child Matters, an organization advocating for children, has monitored this issue. Theodore Roosevelt presided over the first White House Congress on Children, which offered recommendations for the Children's Bureau, established in 1912. He was concerned about the orphanages and about sending children out West to be, in effect, property of caretakers. He was dismayed by the growing breakup of families. The conference led to frontier nurses who visited homes in remote areas to head off medical-related problems that split families. Franklin Delano Roosevelt fostered laws to prevent the continuation of exploitation of young children forced into the labor market. He also had social security programs to protect children and fostered a baseline income security for families to adequately meet the basic needs of children. Thus, standards were set to protect children. Harry Truman set up school lunch programs connecting nutrition health and school progress. Lyndon Johnson, a teacher himself who had worked with poor children, vowed to change the lives of needy children and families that he had seen firsthand. This is reflected in the Lyndon Johnson Library on the campus of the University of Texas at Austin. Johnson led efforts in Head Start programs for preschool children, which currently serve fewer than 5 percent of eligible infants and toddlers due to lack of funding. This pressure certainly adds to the stress on families that is conducive to greater child maltreatment. Children a year or two older are only funded for less than half of their number.

Richard Nixon was perhaps underrated in his assistance to poor families in the passing of the Women's, Infant's, and Children's (WIC) Program for underserved pregnant women. According to

Every Child Matters, we are still the only country in the industrialized world that doesn't have a guaranteed heath and financial program for families, and hundreds of thousands of women and babies do not receive basic care. Where is the outcry about this factor in the equation of child maltreatment?

President Bill Clinton, despite a tsunami of opposition, was able to scratch out a program that reduced the numbers of children with no health care insurance. Nonetheless, after Clinton's term, according to Every Child Matters, there were seven million children lacking health insurance, three million neglected and abused children yearly (an underestimate), sixteen million children in poverty, five million without school-readiness programs, and fifteen million children unsupervised while parents worked. Clinton was willing to consider ratifying the United Nations Bill of Rights for Children, but the opposition from the other side of the aisle derailed this effort.

UNEQUAL TREATMENT OF CHILDREN

When the headlines shout about and point at the child protection services (at times rightly so) for failing children, the curious lack of press about the gross failure of our legislators to protect underserved children is conspicuous by its denial. Who needs to read the research on how, when poverty and unemployment rise, there is more child maltreatment? This also occurs when the military deploys soldiers, and the parent left at home is more likely to maltreat his or her child.

Twenty-seven years ago, Maurer and Wallerstein wrote, "Now in 1987, physical punishment is considered too severe for felons, murderers, criminals of all kinds and ages, including juvenile delinquents, too demeaning for soldiers, servants and spouses. But it remains legal and acceptable for children who are innocent of any crime."[142]

The military (US Marine Corps) was permitted to beat supervisees, but this changed as well, and now it is not legal at all in order to avoid hurting men who "bruise too easily." The US Navy stopped the practice way back in 1853. Marines, I guess, are not as tough as children. The last year that physically punishing prisoners was permitted was 1952. Maurer and Wallerstein (1987) state that you cannot use "the good old days" comparison that society was so much more civil when children were beaten even more. What does one say about the racist lynching and crime-ridden Wild West? Thieves and highway robbers ruled the roost. In "the good old days," discrimination and violence were visited upon new ethnic groups who appeared different and more vulnerable. In the states where school corporal punishment is legal, children with differences such as disabilities and different skin colors receive a disproportionate amount of the corporal punishment in schools and at home, for that matter.

In 1863, when slavery ended (supposedly), so did the physical punishment of slaves. The movie *Lincoln* demonstrated the courage it takes to stop such a practice, which is sorely lacking for our most vulnerable: children. In 1866, after the American Civil War, the US Senate approved Joint Resolution 153 to end corporal punishment of freed men, who many times were punished as if slavery was not ended by the Civil War.[143] Nearly 200 years later, those same states that had slaves (and a few others) are still physically punishing mostly black or disabled schoolchildren in greater numbers proportionately than any other group. In some areas, we have regressed since the late 1860s.

Many serious injuries occur when children are physically punished at school, but President George H.W. Bush fought to have educators who beat these children exempt from liability. He and other (mostly) conservatives have allowed children to be the only citizens in the United States who are permitted to be physically punished by law. This would be a civil rights violation, except children cannot vote. The government, over 160 years ago, had the sense to realize that the Freedman's Bureau and the US Navy, among other groups, had too many preconceived ideas to trust them to physically punish vulnerable citizens in flux.

Consider *The Way We Never Were* by Stephanie Coontz as a backdrop.[144] In the 1960s, I dated a young woman who told me that she wound up and crisply smacked a child whom she was babysitting in the face for disobeying her. I remember showing or feeling no reaction to this beating she described. In the era when we were spanked and physically punished by adults, there was a massive minimizing of the extent of violence in families. No wonder many people dismiss their experiences of physical punishment as children; if I were not in therapy, I might continue to do the same thing. "Beneath the polished facades of many 'ideal' families, suburban as well as urban, was violence, terror or simply grinding misery come to light," observes Coontz. "In the 1950s wife battering was not considered a real crime by most people." Even "feminism expert" Helen Deutsch attributed a great deal of battering to a woman's masochism.[145] In the '50s and '60s, a recurring Jackie Gleason line from *The Honeymooners* was, "One of these days, Alice, pow...in the kisser," delivered with a balled-up fist in her face. Since children are frequently abused in the middle of domestic violence, these media scenes of the fifties are particularly troubling.

Dr. Amy Gutmann, president of the University of Pennsylvania at the time this was written, is a renowned expert on democracy and the development of governments and education. Dr. Gutmann notes that teachers in New York City about fifty years ago were opposed to stopping corporal punishment of children. This included "caning the children on the head."[146] In recent years, corporal punishment has been outlawed in New York schools by the state. She points out that while the teachers' union never supported corporal punishment, with their policy of protecting teachers' jobs at all costs, it was almost impossible to terminate the minority of teachers who were extremely incompetent, which was also a danger to the children. However incompetent (or competent) teachers are, for that matter, educators permitted by law to physically hit children would still be worse.

Furthermore, unions and policies aside, history is not on the side of unbridled corporal punishment. It was established from research that Holocaust victims, often through *bodily*, behavioral, or emotional cues, pass on some of the anxieties they experienced (as per studies at New York University by Rachel Yehuda, 2000).[147] Also, PTSD victims from the military or other traumatized individuals are likely to project their emotional states onto their children. This does affect parenting, and how many teachers come from such families with histories of unresolved trauma? It is clear that there are too many gray areas to allow teachers to have a green light on using corporal punishment with their charges.

WHAT CHILD DEVELOPMENT EXPERTS SAY

Over fifty years ago, Dr. Rudolph Dreikers co-authored a classic book, *Children, the Challenge*. Dr. Dreikers was a disciple of Dr. Alfred Adler, who broke from Freud and emphasized cooperation and the skills needed to attain this goal. He states that "parents relieve their own feelings of frustration when spanking a child." Often a power struggle ensues, and the child has received attention and a sense of power when he is able to have a parent strike out at him.[148] He cites a mother who spanked her child when he was slow to bowel train and defecated in his father's hat. Eminent behaviorist expert on toilet training Dr. Nathan Azrin (1986) is totally opposed to any type of corporal punishment and states how it negatively affects training a child in toilet habits. This is also the view of B.F. Skinner, the renowned pioneer behaviorist.

Azrin wrote a lot against the practice of physically punishing children. He cites another example of a four-year-old boy whose mother spanked him when he urinated on the floor.[149] The result? He kept escalating this habit. Azrin has a chapter entitled "Take Time to Train." This requires patience and anticipating the tasks a child has to learn. If there is a positive, cooperative environment of learning in which the child is supported and not discouraged by too much negativity, the chances of power struggles escalating are lessened.

In 1959, Dr. Thelma Fraiberg authored *The Magic Years,* a classic in the field, in which she wrote that she would have to work gingerly with groups of parents since mentioning anything opposing spanking would bring back painful emotional experiences for the parents and relived memories.[150] Nonetheless, she actively advocated against corporal punishment of children in a respectful, dignified manner. She said, "I do not intend to spank parents…When the speaker takes a position against spanking, all the parents who spank feel as if they are being spanked by the lecturer."

I delicately mention Dr. Benjamin Spock here, as he probably brings up the most negative reactions by pro-spankers. Dr. Spock originally did not oppose "reasonable" spanking but changed his position as research and his experience in the field grew. More recently, there is quite a list of prominent researchers and therapists who changed their minds about corporal punishment as the research grew. Dr. Russell Barkeley, considered perhaps the foremost expert on attention deficit disorder in the United States, changed his recommendations several years ago to tell parents he does not recommend corporal punishment/spanking anymore for children who do not cooperate with time-outs.[151] Experience, research, and public views on this type of parental behavior were reasons for his change. F. Cline and J. Fay have also written in their more recent books that they are now opposed to corporal punishment of children based on the research and their own growing experience with children.[152]

Drs. James Comer and Alvin Poussaint, professors of psychiatry at Yale and Harvard, respectively, and renowned African-American child development experts, appeal to black families to eliminate physical punishment from their repertoire, as this exacerbates tense situations as opposed to working them through with skills that can be learned.

Dr. Poussaint is a long-time advocate of nonphysical methods of setting limits in teaching black children. *Come On, People*, which he and Dr. William Cosby (yes, *that* Bill Cosby) wrote, provides many examples of alternative ways to handle misbehaving children.[153]

There is the 2014 Academy Award–winning movie that had just hit the theaters in late 2013 entitled *Twelve Years a Slave*. The director,

Steve McQueen, is British and black. He tells how slavery is in our midst even today in the guise of child labor excesses, human trafficking, poverty, drugs, and subpar education. He further states, "I used to be beaten with a belt and a lot of people did it in those days because it was perpetuated from slavery." But it is still done in *these* days! Also, as many antispanking groups point out, the main areas where school corporal punishment is legal are the states of the South, where slavery had the strongest foothold. The writings of J. Comer[154], as well as Drs. Poussaint and Cosby, also reflect this factor.

McQueen mentions how the story of Solomon Northrup, who wrote a memoir about his travails as a free black man forced into slavery, and other such historical occurrences receive negligible exposure in US history books. He said that, deservedly, Anne Frank's memoirs have received great ongoing publicity and that similarly stories such as Northrup's need to be thrust into the public eye as a significant part of history as well.

CHAPTER 10

CONCLUSION

James Fallon, in *The Psychopath Inside: A Neuroscientist's Personal Journey into the Dark Side of the Brain,* relates that he, as a successful neuroscientist and caring husband and father, always felt that he struggled to be empathetic and was prone to taking risky adventures and not caring much what people thought.[155] He was an x-ray worker in the hospital who was immersed in the discoveries deep in the brain and body well before he went into the field of psychology and pursued a PhD in neuroscience. Fallon was asking questions about the brains of psychopaths for years and, as a neuroscientist, had the skills and background in x-ray technology to do some serious work. In the process, he had an image made of his own brain and found that it had the characteristics of a psychopath with activities strongly focused in the more primitive region of the brain.

He was a student of epigenetics (the science of the interaction between genetics and the environment) and found that his warm, loving family gave him the support that he needed to not fall into the more criminal and sinister aspects of his personality. He has memories of his needs being met and a secure attachment to his mother and father. This included reasoning and support when he was being corrected. He recognized that others with this brain structure were often not as fortunate. A harsh, punitive environment could have interacted with his predisposition to antisocial behavior and sent him into this negative pattern. He, like the Oliners, recognizes the power of the interaction between hereditary predisposition and the environment in which one finds oneself.

My mother, unlike Dr. Fallon, did not receive the parental support that would have enabled her to handle conflict without hurting others. In the twilight of her ninety-two years, my mother realized that she spanked because that was all she knew, and it became a toxic pattern; in her last letters, she apologized for it, although my brother and I had made our peace with her well before she passed. It was my parents who allowed and even encouraged me to go for years of psychotherapy, and that saved my life. The first psychiatrist who saw me when I was age eighteen said that without therapy, my life wouldn't be worth five cents. I feel fortunate to have parents who could admit they were not able to provide nurturance and could allow others to help me. As a therapist myself, I often found that when a child was making progress, this could be threatening to the parents, and they could sabotage or pull the child out of therapy. Changing patterns of generations of families is ominous. Over the ages, progress has been glacial, but it is much too slowly evolving in the United States.

This book is only an offshoot work of advocates dating back to Quintillian, founding father Benjamin Rush, and some unsung heroes in the last forty years. Jordan Riak has, for decades, maintained an encyclopedic website containing literally thousands of research studies and articles from the media and prominent figures. He has written countless letters fighting to change school corporal punishment. Because of him, many state laws have changed. Probably the most significant was California, where Riak did the lion's share of the work. I wrote a letter added to his archives regarding a book by former *Psychology Today* editor, radio host, and Harvard PhD Robert Epstein. Dr. Epstein had trained psychologists, according to his account, to teach their clients therapeutic skills for nonphysical punishment in a series of courses they needed for their license credits. He later did an about-face in his book *The Case against Adolescence,* where he wrote that despite the brutal nature of physical punishment, it is a necessary tool in the parents' bag of skills. He also wrote that he supported school corporal punishment. My letter challenging this position was written out of sadness that such a learned man would change his mind in the process of selling a book.

Paula Flowe, leader of the organization The Hitting Stops Here, spent years traveling around the country, vociferously advocating for an end to school corporal punishment. She was the spark behind campaigns that included media and billboards, which she somehow brought to the public despite a bare-bones budget.

Nadine Block, leader of the Center for Effective Discipline, has a website with countless articles on the topic and examples of many alternative techniques to corporal punishment. She was a leader in the state of Ohio, voting to end school corporal punishment.

Dr. George Holden, a psychology professor from Southern Methodist University, has written numerous research articles on the negative impact of physical punishment. He arranged a summit of advocates from around the world to come to Dallas to share ideas and plan strategies to challenge child physical punishment. As mentioned, the Methodist religion departed from its early leader John Wesley's position of the need for intense physical punishment, even with babies, to exorcise their original sins and break their wills.

Robbyn Peters-Bennett developed a comprehensive website in the fields of advocacy and protecting children from physical punishment and utilizes interactive communication in an ongoing manner.

There are too many advocates to cover them all, including many from around the world and the architects of the United Nations Bill of Children's Rights. A group of these advocates, including me, called the office of Arne Duncan, the secretary of education, about setting up a bill to erase the legality of school corporal punishment for all states. The Department of Education began presenting this as a civil rights issue. Congressperson Carolyn McCarthy of New York courageously entered a bill twice to end this legalized child abuse in schools. In 2010 and again in 2011, these bills died in committee without even being properly debated, and Congress did not have an opportunity to even cast a vote. In my opinion, this was a major blow to the cause, from which we are still regrouping. This book is partially driven by this frustration.

Please note in June 2014 a new bill, HR 5005, has been proposed to end school corporal punishment. There is more information about the bill, a deadline date for it to be decided, and how to advocate the bill on website stoplegalchildabuse.com which is mine.

CONCLUSION

To conclude, I would like to return to the book's beginning quote from Dr. Oz:

First and foremost we do not believe in spanking because it hasn't been shown to be effective in changing behavior, because it's allowing parents to vent their own stress, and because it teaches your child to be more aggressive to others (mirror neurons, people)! That's not to mention the fact that spanking is associated in some research with lower IQs in people.[156]

After Dr. Oz recommended a certain brand of popcorn with olive oil found in Trader Joe's, I hustled there, but hundreds of bags had already been purchased, and none were left. The same thing happened with sriracha, a very spicy condiment he advocated. After that, I went to stores all over Philadelphia and New Jersey, but they were sold out, showing that the public trusts and adores Dr. Oz. Unfortunately, this adoration appears to stop cold with his vehement advocacy to never spank children. Maybe we will learn a compassionate way to deal with children from "the Wizard of Oz" yet and from countless other researchers, clinicians, and a legion of parent mensches.

Dr Oz was invited by Rabbi Schmuely Boteach, who opposed the concept of children's original sin, to visit Yad Vashem, the Holocaust Museum in Israel. The men visited with their families. Dr Oz was mystified by the arguments the Nazis used to justify their crimes against Israel. He said, "The lessons of the Holocaust should be remembered, so that history does not repeat itself." This is an argument this book focuses on through the lens of child corporal punishment.

WORKS CITED

Adorno, T. M., E. Frenkel-Brunswick, D. J. Levinson, and N. S. Sanford. (1982). *The Authoritarian Personality*. New York: Norton.

Alward, M. M. (2013). "Is Your Child's Teacher a Bully?" Accessed November 19, 2013.http://www.Allwardlocalschool directory.com.

Amreim, S. (June 14, 2013). "Relatives Urge Florida to Issue Exhumations at School." Accessed November 7, 2013. http://jabout.reuters.comm/jfulllegal.

Arendt, H. (2003).*The Portable Hannah Arendt*. New York: Penguin.

"After 148 Years Mississippi Ratifies 13th Amendment Ban on Slavery." (February, 2013). *The Carion Ledger*.

Axness, M. (2012). *Parenting for Peace: Raising the Next Generation of Peacemakers*. Boulder, CO: Sentier.

Aymond, G. in B. Nolan. (2011). *Times-Picayune*.

Azrin, N.H, and R. M. Fox. (1986). *Toilet Training in Less than a Day*. New York: Pocket.

Books, Babbit, F.C., ed. (1977). *Plutarch: Moralia, The Education of Children and the Young Man Studying Poetry.* London: Loeb Classical Library.

Bachrach, S. (April 25, 2013). "Some Were Neighbors: Collaborators and Complicity During the Holocaust." *Gillette News.*

Beane, A. L. (2012). *Bully-Free Classroom.* Minneapolis: Free Spirit Publishing.

"Benjamin Rush Speaks His Mind." (October 2, 2009). Samuel Gilgal (blog). Word Press.com.

Barkley, R. (2013). *Your Defiant Child: 8 Steps to Better Behavior.* New York: Guilford.

Bonnett, R. P. (Feb. 2013). "Parent Education." http: Jjwp. mejPUER-ol.

Berman, J. (2010). *Superbaby.* New York: Sterling

Bettelheim, B. (1987). *A Good Enough Parent: A Book on Child Rearing.* New York: Random House.

———. (2013). "Quotations." Accessed November 7, 2013.http:// www. izquotes.com.

Boehm, C. (2012). *Moral Origins: The Evolution of Virtue, Altruism and Shame.* New York: Perseus.

Boteach, S. (2012). *Kosher Jesus.* Jerusalem: Geffen.

Brain World. (Spring 2010). *Beliefs and Values That Changed Education Since 1965: Change in Beliefs and Values 1990–2010.* United Nations International Education Association.

Brazelton, T.B. (2013). *Learning to Listen: A Life of Caring for Children.* Boston: DeCapo.

Brazelton T.B., and M. Strauss, M. (1999). "Is It Time to Ban Corporal Punishment of Children?" *Canadian Medical Association Journal* 161: 861–62.

Brehl, R. (2013). "For the Health of Our Society: 'Normal' Child Abuse Prevention." *Psychology Central.*

Brent, D., and M. Silverstein. (May 1, 2013). "1777–1778. Shedding Light on the Long Shadow of Childhood Adversity." *JAMA* 309, no. 17: 861–62.

Brohl, K. (2013). *Social Service Workplace Bullying: Betrayal of Good Intentions.* New York: Lyceum.

Brown, A., and D. Fields. (2011). *Baby 411.* Colorado: Windser Peak Press.

Callahan, J. (1992). *Do What He Says He's Crazy.* New York: Quill.

Callahan, R. (Feb. 18, 2013). "Oh Mississippi: Who Knew Slavery Was Never Really Ratified until This Month? *Clutch: Daily News Letter.*

Caring for Our Children: Nation Health and Safety Performance Standards, Guideline of Out of Home Programs. (2011). Washington, DC: American Pediatric Association.

Carter, G. (June 8, 2004). "Advocacy Groups Link Paddling to Slavery. University of Alabama: *The Exponent Student Newspaper.*

Chaucer, S. (2006). "Teaching Children the Importance of the Holocaust." Yahoo Contributer Network. Accessed Feb. 7, 2013.

Chesler, P. (2011). *Mothers on Trial for Children and Custody.* Chicago: Lawrence Hill Books.

Chopra, D., and R. Tanzi.(2011). *Super Brain.* New York: Random House.

"Classics from the Comics." (Aug. 11, 2010). Network 54. Accessed October 16, 2013.

Cleaver, S. (2013). *Why Are We Still Hitting?* New York: Scholastic Press.

Cline, F., and J. Kay.(2006). *Parenting with Love and Logic.* Colorado Springs: Nav Press.

Collier, G. (2012). *Everything Is Bigger in Texas: How the Lone Star State Hijacked the American Agenda.* New York: Norton.

Colorado Accomodation Model.. *Building Bridges for the Future.* Colorado Department of Education.www.cde.state.co.us/ cdesped/building brides. (2013).

Cooperson, D. (2007). Child Abuse and Neglect: Effects on the Brain and a Call to Action.Child Welfare Section Connection. National Association of Social Workers. Issue 2. 6-8

Cooperson, D.(2009). Children's Rights, Social Work Values and Corporal Punishment. Child Welfare Section Connection. National Association of Social Workers. Issue 2. 2,8- 9.

Cooperson, D. (2007-8). Advocacy for Children Backed by Latest Science Needed Now More Than Ever. The Pennsylvania Social Worker. 29,3.

Cosby, W., and A. Poussaint. (2007). *Come on, People*. New York: Thomas Nelson.

Comer, J. (2004). *Leave No Child Behind: Preparing Today's Children for Tomorrow's World*. New York: Children's Defense Fund.

Coontz, S. (1993). *The Way We Never Were*. New York: Basic.

Cotler. I. (2011). "Lessons Learned from the Holocaust. Aish.com." http://www.   Aish/ho/i/7_Lessons_from_the_Holocaust. html.

Cotton, L. (1971). "Is There Enough Laughter in Your Life?" Dr. Mardy's Blog. Accessed October 24, 201. www.iwise. comdmardyblog

Cozolino, L. (2013). *The Social Neuroscience of Education: Optimizing Learning and Attachment in the Classroom*. New York: Norton.

Crandall, J., and E. Vida. (2010). "Support for Spanking: Most Americans Think Corporal Punishment Is O.K." ABC News.com.

Cusac, M.(2009). *Cruel and Unusual Punishment: The Culture of Punishment in America*. New Haven: Yale.

Daily Mail Reporter. (June 16, 2012). "Hit Him Harder: Teacher Forced 20 Kindergarten Students to Line up and Hit Classmate Accused of Being a Bully." Mail Online.

Davidson, J., and R. Yehuda. (2000). *Clinical Manual on Post Traumatic Stress Disorder.* New York. Science Press, Inc.

Davis, N., S. Clark, M. Davis, and G. Freed. (March 14, 2011). "Father's Depression Related to Positive and Negative Parenting Behaviors with 1 Year Old Children." Pediatrics online.www.ncbl.nim.nih.gov/pubmed/21402627

deLench, B. (2006). *Home Team Advantage: Critical Role of Moms in Team Sports.* New York: Harper Collins.

DeMauss, J. (1975). *The History of Childhood.* New York: Harper and Row.

De Zulueta, F. (2006). *From Pain to Violence: The Traumatic Roots of Destructiveness.* Hoboken, NJ: Wiley.

Dobson, J. (2003). *Parent Answer Book.* Illinois: Tyndale.

Domestic Violence Resource Center. (2013). Hillsboro Colorado: NetRaising.www.dvrc.org

Doty, M. (November 14, 2013). "*12 Years a Slave* Underscores Scourge of Modern Slavery." Yahoo Movies website.

Dreikurs, R., and V. Stolz. (1990). *Children, the Challenge.* New York: Penguin.

Eddy, M., and A. Rizzo. (March10, 2010). "Pope's Brother Knew of Beatings." Boston.com.

Ember, C. R., and M. Ember. (2005). "Explaining Corporal Punishment to Children: A Cross Culture Study. *American Anthropologist* 107: 609–17.

Epstein, R. (2007). *The Case Against Adolescence: Rediscovering the Adult in Every Adult.* Sanger, CA: Quill.

Fathman, R. (November 2, 2003). "Prohibiting Corporal Punishment Beneficial." *Pacific News.*

Felitti, V. J., et al. (1998). "Relationship of Childhood Abuse and Household Dysfunction to Many Leading Causes of Death in Adults: The Adverse Experience (ACE) Study." *American Journal of Preventive Medicine* 14: 245–2.

Fields, D., and Brown, A. (2004). *Baby 411.* London: Windser Peak Press.

Fleishman, S. M. (1905). *The History of the Jewish Foster Home and Orphan Asylum.* Michigan: Board of Managers.

Flynn, C.P. (1999). Exploring the Link Between Corporal Punishment and Children's Cruelty to Animals. Journal of Marriage and the Family. 61,971-981

Fogelman, E. (1994). *Conscious and Courage: Rescuers of the Jews during the Holocaust.* New York: Anchor.

Fraiberg, S. H. (1996). *The Magic Years: Understanding and Handling Problems of Early Childhood.* New York: Fireside.

Friedman, D. A., (2005). *Jewish Pastoral Care: A Practical Handbook from Traditional and Contemporary Resources.* New York: Jewish Lights.

Friel, J., and D. O. Friel. (2012). *The Power and Grace of Nasty and Nice.* Deerfield Beach: HCL.

"Founding Father Benjamin Rush Speaks His Mind." (October 6, 2009). Samuel Gilgal Blog. Word Press.Com. www.samuelat-gilgal.wordpress/2009/founding-father

Garberino, J., and E. deLara. (2002). *Words Can Hurt Forever.* New York: Free Press.

Gellar, T. (2007). *The Loved Dog: The Nonaggressive Way to Teach Your Dog Good Behavior.* New York: Simon and Shuster.

George, T. D. (2013). *Untangling the Mind.* New York: Harper.

Gerhardt, S. (2010). *The Selfish Society: How We All Forgot to Love and Made Money Instead.* London: Simon and Schuster.

Gershoff, E. (2010). "More Harm Than Good: A Summary of the Research on the Intended and Unintended Effects of Corporal Punishment." *Law and Contemporary Problems* 73, no.31: 3156.

Giles-Sims, J. (1985). "A Longitudinal Study of Battered Children of Battered Wives." *Family Relations* 34, no. 2: 205–10.

Gilligan, J. (1996). *Violence: Reflections on a National Epidemic.* New York: Vintage.

Ginott, H. (1961). *Between Parent and Child.* New York: MacMillam.

Gottlieb, D. (Dec. 2013) In R. Chillott. "Do I Make You Uncomfortable?" *Psychology Today* 46, no. 6: 77.

Gonnerman, J. (Aug. 20, 2007). "School of Shock." *Mother Jones.*

Gottman, J., and N. Jacobson. (2011). *When Men Batter Women.* New York: Simon and Schuster.

Greven, P. (1990). *Spare the Child: The Religious Roots of Punishment and Psychological Impact of Physical Abuse.* New York: Vintage.

Grey, P. (2012). *Free to Learn.* New York: Basic.

Grille, R. (2005). *Parenting for a Peaceful World.* Australia: Longueville Press.

Gross-Loh, C. (2013). *Parenting without Borders.* New York: Avery.

Hart, C. (2013). *High Price.* New York: Harper.

Heffernan, M. (2011). *Willful Blindness: Why We Ignore the Obvious.* New York: Walker.

Heimlich, J. (2011). *Breaking Their Will: Shedding Light on Religious Maltreatment*. Amherst, Prometheus.

Hobson, R. P., and A. Lee. (1999). "Imitation and Identification in Autism." *Journal of Child Psychiatry and Psychology* 40: 649–59.

Hogg, T. (2013). *Secrets of the Baby Whisperer for Toddlers*. New York: Ballantine.

Hunt, I. A. (2006). *On Hitler's Mountain*. New York: Harper Perennial.

Hyman, L., and P. Snook. (1999). *The Case Against Spanking: How to Discipline Your Child without Hitting*. New York: Wiley.

Iacoboni, M. (2009). *Mirroring People: The Science of Empathy and How We Connect with Others*. New York: Farrar Strauss.

Jacobson, N. and G. Gottman. (2007). *When Men Batter Women: New Insights into Ending Abusive Relationships*. New York: Simon and Schuster.

Janis, I. (1982). *Groupthink*. Boston: Wadsworth.

Jeffrey, C. (April12, 2012). Video: Teen Is Tied *Down*, Shocked by Teacher at School for Autistic Kids. *Mother Jones*.

Joyce, K. (2013). *The Child Catchers*. New York: Public Affairs.

Kagan, J., and S. Snidman. (2004). *The Long Shadow of Temperament*. Boston: Harvard University Press.

Kagan, R. (2004). *Rebuilding Attachments with Traumatized Children: Healing from Losses, Violence, Abuse, and Neglect.* New York: Haworth Press.

Kaplan, L. (2013). "Spare the Rod and Spoil the Child. Temple Israel, Wilkes Barre, PA, Ohio: Center for Effective Discipline.

Karp, H. (2002). *The Happiest Baby on the Block.* New York: Bantam.

———. (2008). *The Happiest Toddler on the Block.* New York: Bantam.

Katrrandjian, O. (2012). "'If Fred got two beatings a day' homework asks." ABC News. Retrieved on 1/7/13.

Kaufman, G., W. Lipschitz, and D. Setel. (2000). "Responding to Domestic Violence." In D. Friedman, ed. *Jewish Pastoral Care.* Woodstock, VT: Jewish Lights.

Kazdin, A. (2013). *Everyday Parenting Toolkit.* New York: Houghton Mifflin.

Keeshan, B. (Nov., Dec. 1988). "Corporal Punishment." *Humanist* 39:10–12.

Kempe, H., E. H. Keifer, and R. D. Krugman. (1997). *The Battered Child.* Chicago: University of Chicago Press.

Larue, A. (2011). *Unequal Childhoods.* Berkeley: Berkeley Press.

Lee, S., and E. T. Gershoff. "Does Warmth Moderate Longitudinal Association between Maternal Spanking and

Aggression in Early Childhood?" *Developmental Psychology.*
doi:10.1037ja0031630.

Leventhal, J. M., and J. M. Gaither. (2012). "Injuries Due to Child
Abuse on the Rise. *Pediatrics* 130, no. S:26–27.

Lorber, M. F., and B. Egeland. (2009). "Infancy Parenting and
Externalizing Psychopathology from Childhood to
Adulthood." *Developmental Psychology* 45: 909–12.

Lifton, R. J.(1988). *The Nazi Doctors: Medical Killings and the Psychology
of Genocide.* New York: Basic.

Marzano, R. J., J. S. Marzano, and D. J. Pickering. (2003). *Classroom
Management That Works: Research-Based Strategies for Every
Teacher.* Alexandria, Association for Supervision and
Curriculum Development.

Mason, K. I. (2013). *Bullying No More.* Hauppauge, NY: Barrons.

Mather, C. (2012). *The Well-Ordered Family.* New York: Soli Deo
Gloria Publishers.

Maurer, A,. and J. S. Wallerstein. (1984). *The Bible and Rod: Alternatives
to Corporal Punishment.* Vol. 1. Berkeley: Generation Books.

Mayer, L. M., and Blome. (2013). "The Importance of Early
Targeted Intervention: The effect of Maternal and Child
Characteristics on the Use of Corporal Punishment on the
Use of Physical Discipline." *Journal of Behavior and Social
Environment* 23: 144–58.

Mayer, L. M., and B. Thursby. (2012). "Adolescent Parents and Their Children: A Multifaceted Approach to Prevention on Adverse Childhood Experiences (ACE)." *Journal of Prevention Intervention in the Community.* Washington, DC: The Catholic University, PubMed.

Maxim, H. (1999). *A Genius in the Family: Through a Small Son's Eyes.* London: Akadine Press.

McCall, R. and C. Groark. (2000). "The Future of Child Development and Social Policy." *Child Development* 71, no. 1: 197–204.

McCrackin, O. (2011). "Depressed Dads More Likely to Spank Kids." Psych Central. http://psychcentral.com/newsj16depressed-dads-more-likely-to-kids /24436/html.

McHugh, M. (1994). Bellevue Hospital Focus Group.

Mead, M., and R. Metra. (2000). *Study Culture at a Distance.* Chicago: Berghahn.

Milgram, S. (1974). *Obedience to Authority.* New York: Harper.

Miller, A. (2006). *The Body Never Lies: The Lingering Effects of Hurtful Parenting.* New York: Norton.

Murkoff, E., and A. Eisenberg. (2010). *What to Expect the First Year.* New York: Pocket Books.

National Health and Safety Performance Standards: Guidelines for Out of Home Child Care Placements. (1992).Washington DC:

American Public Health Association, National Center for Education in Maternal and Child Health.

News on Japan.com. (2013). "6,721 Teachers across Japan Use Corporal Punishment." The Japan News.net. newsonjapan. com/html/newsdesk/103985.php

Nolan, B. (December 23, 2011). "St. Augustine Board Struggle Is Settled: Paddling Is Banned." *Times Picayune.*

Oliner. S. (2003). *Do Unto Others: How Altruism Inspires True Acts of Courage. Cambridge: Westview.*

Oliner, S., and P. Oliner. (1988). *The Altruistic Personality: Rescuers of Jews in Nazi Germany.* New York: Free Press.

Pagelow, M. D., and L. Pagelow. (1984). *Family Violence.* New York: Praeger.

Partnow, E. B., ed. (2007). *The Quotable Jewish Woman.* VT: Jewish Lights.

Paolantonio, S. (2008). *How Football Changes America.* Chicago: Triumph.

Pearl, M., and D. Pearl. (1997). *No Greater Joy.* Tennessee: No Greater Joy Ministries.

Perry, B. D., and M. Szalavitz. (2006). *The Boy Who Was Raised as a Dog and Other Stories from a Psychiatrist's Notebook: What Traumatized Children Can Teach us About Loss, Love and Healing.* New York: Basic Books.

———. (2010). *Born for Love: Why Empathy Is Essential and Endangered.* New York: HarperCollins.

Petit, M. (2012). *Presidents Helping Children.* Washington, DC: Every Child Matters Education Fund.

Pincus, S. H., R. House, J. Christenson, and L. E. Adler. (2007). "The Emotional Cycle of Deployment: A Military Family Perspective." *Journal of Army Medical Department*: 615–23.

Pinker, S. (2012). *The Better Angels of Our Nature: Why Violence Has Declined.* New York: Viking.

Plutarch. *Moralia 1*(1927).Boston: Harvard University Press.

Pring, R. (1984). *Personal and Social Education in the Curriculum.* London: Hoddard and Stoughton.

Quintillian. (May 31, 2009). "Quotations Showing Diverse Opinions. Ontario Consultants on Religious Tolerance.

Redford, R. C. (2010). *Crazy: My Seven Years at Bruno Bettelheim's Orthogenic School.* Bloomington: Trafford Publishing.

Reich, S., E. Penner, G. Duncan, and A. Auger. (2003). "Using Baby Books to Change New Mother's Attitude about Corporal Punishment and Child Neglect." *Child Abuse and Neglect* 36: 108–17.

Reiner, S. (2013). *Kafka: The Years of Insight.* Princeton: Princeton University Press.

Resnick, S. K. (2013). *You Saved Me Too: What the Holocaust Taught Me about Living, Dying, Loving, and Swearing in Yiddish.* Connecticut: Skirt.

Ritvo, E., J. Q. DelRosso, and C. LaRiche. (Aug. 13, 2011). "Psychosocial Judgments and Perceptions with Acne Vulgaris: A Blinded Controlled Comparison of Adult and Peer Evaluations." *Biosocial Medicine* 5, no. 1. 11doi 10:1186/1751-0759-5-11.

Rosemond, J. (1989). *Six Points for Raising Happy Healthy Children.* Kansas City: Andrews and McMeel.

———. (2006). *The Well-Behaved Child: Discipline That Really Works.* Kansas City: Andrews and McMeel.

———. (2009). *Toilet Training without Tantrums.* Nashville: Thomas Nelson.

———. (2012). *Parent Babble: How Parents Can Recover from Fifty Years of Bad Advice.* Kansas City: McMeel and Andrews.

Ross, C. (1989). South Suicidal National Center. Burlington, VA.

Ross, C. (March/April 1988). In Hembree, D. "The Tragic Side of Classroom Punishment." *Hippocrates.*

Roth, E. (April 25, 2013). "Bystanders Not So Innocent." *New York Times.*

Scaer, R. (2001). *The Body Bears the Burden: Trauma, Dissociation, and Disease.* Binghamton: Haworth.

———. (2005). *The Trauma Spectrum: Hidden Wounds and Human Resiliency.* New York: Norton.

Schade, V. (2013). *Secrets of a Dog Trainer.* New York: Wiley.

Scott, G. R. (1938). *The History of Corporal Punishment.* London: T.W. Laurie Ltd.

Severe, S. (2011). *How to Behave so Your Preschoolers Will Too.* New York: Viking.

Shin, E. U. (Fall 2010). "The Happy School Campaign in South Korea." *Brain World* 1, no. 4: 48–49.

Siegel, B. (2003). *Helping Children with Autism Learn.* London: Oxford.

Siegel, D., and T. P. Bryson. (2003). *The Whole Brain Child.* New York: Delacorte.

Siegel, S., and L. Edwards. (2000). *An Orphan in New York.* New York: Xlibris.

Simons, D. D., and S. K. Wurtele. (2010). "Relations between Parents' Use of Corporal Punishment and Their Endorsement of Spanking and Hitting." *Child Abuse and Neglect* 34: 639–46.

Smith, M., J. A. Hubbard, and J. P. Laurenceau (2011). "Profiles of Anger in Second-Grade Children: Examination of Self-Report, Observational and Physiological Components." *Journal of Experimental Child Psychology* 110: 213–26.

Smith, M. et al. (1997). *Research on Parental Behavior.* London: Thomas Coram Research Unit, University of London Institute of Education.

Steiner, R. (2013). *Kafka: The Years of Insight.* Princeton: Princeton Press.

Stern, K. (2013). *With Charity for All: Why Charities Are Failing and a Better Way to Give.* New York: Doubleday.

Stoller, R. J. (1994). *On the Development of Masculinity and Femininity.* New York: Science.

———. (1975). *Perversion: The Erotic Form of Hatred.* London: Karnak.

Storm, H. (2002). *Go Girl: Raising Happy, Healthy, Confident, and Successful Girls through Sports.* Naperville, IL: Sourcebooks.

Straus, M., and D. A. Donnelly. (2006). *Beating the Devil Out of Them.* London: Transaction.

Strean, S. (1984). *Psychoanalytical Approaches to the Hostile and Violent Client.* New York: Haworth.

Swearer, S. (2013). In E. Bazelon, ed. *Sticks and Stones: Defeating the Culture of Bullying.* New York: Random House.

Teicher, M. (2002). "Scars That Won't Heal: The Neurobiology of Child Abuse." *Scientific American* 286, no. 3: 68–75.

Telushkin, J. (2000). *Jewish Literacy.* New York: Random House.

Twemlow, S. W., P. Fonagy, P. Sacco, and J. R. Brethour. (May 2006). "Teachers Who Bully Students: A Hidden Trauma." *International Journal of Social Psychiatry* 52, no. 3:187–98.

Vromen, S. (2008). *Hidden Children of the Holocaust.* London: Oxford.

Walant, K.B. (1995). "Creating the Capacity for Attachment: Treating Addictions and the Alienated Self." London: Aronson.

West, J. (2011). *West by West: My Charmed Tormented Life.* New York: Little Brown.

White House Conference on Bullying. (March 10, 2011). "New Details: Conference on Bullying Prevention." Washington, DC: Office of the Press Secretary.

Wilson, C. (2010). *Perfect Phrases for School Administrators.* New York: McGraw Hill.

Woodhouse, B. (2008). *Hidden in Plain Sight: The Tragedy of Children's Rights from Franklin to Lionel Tate.* London: Oxford.

Young-Bruel, E. (2012). *Childism: Confronting Prejudice against Children.* New Haven: Yale Press.

Zhou, K. (September 12, 2012). "Alarming! School Bullies Attack Almost Half of Kids with Autism." Takepart. http://www.takepart.com/article/2012/09/04/school-bullies-attack-almost-half-kids-who-have-autism.

Zimmerman, J. (Nov. 29, 2011). "A Bright Line Not Yet Drawn." *Philadelphia Inquirer.*

NOTES

Epigraphs

H. Ginott, *Between Parent and Child* (New York: MacMillan, 1961).

M. F. Roizen and M. Oz, *You Raising Your Child: The Owner's Manual from the First Breath to First Grade* (New York: Free Press, 2010).

Chapter 1: Holocaust and the Safety of Today's Children

[1] J. Heimlich, *Breaking Their Will: Shedding Light on Religious Maltreatment* (Amherst, MA: Prometheus, 2011).

[2] P. Greven, S*pare the Child: The Religious Roots of Punishment and Psychological Impact of Physical Abuse* (New York: Vintage, 1990).

[3] Quintillian, "Quotations Showing Diverse Opinions," Ontario Consultants on Religious Tolerance, May 31, 2009, www.religious-tolerance.org/news.

[4] Plutarch, *Moralia 1* (Boston: Harvard University Press, 1927), 41.

[5] S. Bachrach, "Some Were Neighbors: Collaborators and Complicity During the Holocaust," *Gillette News*, April 25, 2013.

6 R. Fathman, "Prohibiting Corporal Punishment Beneficial," *Pacific News*, Nov. 2, 2003, Accessed Jan. 2, 2014, www.nospank.net/fathman5.htm.

7 S. Oliner and P. Oliner, *The Altruistic Personality: Rescuers of Jews in Nazi Germany (New York:Free Press,1988).*

8 S. Oliner, *Do Unto Others: How Altruism Inspires True Acts of Courage* (Cambridge: Westview, 2003).

9 R. Grille, *Parenting for a Peaceful World* (Australia: Longueville Press, 2005).

10 T. M. Adorno, E. Frenkel-Brunswick, E. Levinson, and D. A. Sandford, *The Authoritarian Personality* (New York: Norton).

11 E. Fogelman, *Conscious and Courage: Rescuers of the Jews during the Holocaust* (New York: Anchor, 1994).

12 J. Korczak, *The Child's Right to Respect: Legacy of Today's Challenges for Children* (London: Council of Europe, 2009).

13 Oliner, 33.

14 I. A. Hunt, *On Hitler's Mountain* (New York: Harpers Perennial, 2006).

15 M. Shatzman, *Soul Murder: Persecution in the Family* (New York: New American Library, 1974).

16 A. Miller, *The Body Never Lies: The Lingering Effects of Hurtful Parenting* (New York: Harper, 2006).

[17] S. K. Resnick, *You Saved Me Too: What the Holocaust Taught Me about Living, Dying, and Swearing in Yiddish* (Connecticut: Skirt, 2013).

[18] B. Bettelheim, "Quotations," Accessed Nov. 17, 2013, http://www.izquotes.com..

[19] B. Bettelheim, *A Good Enough Parent: A Book on Child Rearing* (New York: Random House, 1987).

[20] R. C. Redford, *Crazy: My Seven Years at Bruno Bettelheim's Orthogenic School* (London: Trafford, 2010).

[21] S. Milgram, *Obedience to Authority* (New York: Harper, 1974).

Chapter 2: Why Hasn't the United States Learned from the Holocaust Lessons?

[22] B. Woodhouse, *Hidden in Plain Sight: The Tragedy of Children's Rights from Franklin to Lionel Tate* (London: Oxford, 2008).

[23] L. DeMausse, *The History of Childhood* (New York: Harper, 1975).

[24] Woodhouse.

[25] M. Heffernan, *Willful Blindness: Why We Ignore the Obvious* (New York: Walker, 2011).

[26] I. Cotler, "Lessons Learned from the Holocaust," Aish.com, 2011, http://www.Aish/ho/i/7_Lessons_from_the_Holocaust.html.

[27] S. Chaucer, "Teaching Children the Importance of the Holocaust," Yahoo Contributor Network, 2006.

[28] M. Axness, *Parenting for Peace: Raising the Next Generation of Peacemakers* (Boulder: Sention, 2012).

[29] H. Ginott, *Between Parent and Child* (New York: MacMillan, 1961).

[30] E. Young-Bruehl, *Childism* (New Haven: Yale Press, 2012)

[31] R. J. Lifton, *The Nazi Doctors: Medical Killings and the Psychology of Genocide* (New York: Basic, 1988).

[32] S. Pinker, *The Better Angels of Our Nature: Why Violence Has Declined*: New York: Penguin, 2012).

[33] C. Boehm, *Moral Origins: The Evolution of Virtue, Altruism, and Shame.* New York: Perseus, 2012).

Chapter 3: The Tower of Babble: From Parent Babble to Spanking Babble

[34] J. Rosemond, *Parent Babble: How Parents Can Recover from Fifty Years of Bad Advice* (Kansas City: McMeel and Andrews, 2012).

[35] J. Rosemond, *The Well-Behaved Child: Discipline That Really Works* (Kansas City: Andrews and McMeel, 2006).

[36] J. Rosemond, *Six Points for Raising Happy Healthy Children* (Kansas City: Andrews and McMeel, 1989).

[37] M. Eddy and A. Rizzo, "Pope's Brother Knew of Beatings," Boston: Associated Press, Globe Newspaper Company, Mar. 10, 2010, Boston.com, www.boston.com/.../2010/03/10/popes-brother-knew-of-beatings.

[38] R. Kagan, *Rebuilding Attachments with Traumatized Children: Healing from Losses, Violence, Abuse, and Neglect* (New York: Haworth Press, 2004), 62.

[39] M. Pearl and D. Pearl, *No Greater Joy*. Pleasantville:(Tennessee: No Greater Joy Ministries, 1997).

[40] J. Dobson, *Parent Answer Book* (Illinois: Tyndale, 2003).

[41] M. F. Lorber and Eglang. "Infancy Parenting and Externalizing Psychopathology from Childhood to Adulthood," Developmental Psychology 45 (2009): 909–12.

[42] T. W. Phelan, *123 Magic for Christian Parents* (Ellyn, IL: Parent Magic, 2007).

[43] M. Straus and D. A. Donnelly, *Beating the Devil Out of Them* (London: Transaction, 2006).

[44] S. Boteach, *Kosher Jesus* (Jerusalem: Geffen, 2012).

[45] M. McHugh, Bellevue Hospital Focus Group, 1994.

[46] J. Callahan, *Do What He Says He Is Crazy*. Portland: Quill, 1992).

[47] M. Smith et al.Research on Parental BehaviorLondon: Thomas Coram Research Unit, Institute of Education. University of London. 1997.)

[48] R. Scaer, *The Body Bears the Burden: Dissociation and Disease* (Binghamton: Haworth, 2001).

[49] H. Maxim, *A Genius in the Family: Through a Small Son's Eyes* (London: Akadine Press, 1999).

[50] B. D. Perry and S. Szalavitz, *Born for Love: Why Empathy Is Essential and Endangered* (New York: Harper-Collins, 2010).

[51] J. Rosemond, *Toilet Training without Tantrums* (Nashville: Thomas Nelson, 2009).

[52] J. Schrand and L. Devine, *Outsmarting Anger: 7 Strategies for Defusing Our Most Dangerous Emotion* (San Francisco: Jossey-Bass, 2013).p34

[53] J. Schrand,,p 34

[54] M. Smith, J. A. Hubbard, and J. P. Larenceau, "Profiles of Anger in Second Grade Children: Examination of Self-Report, Observational and Physiological Components," *Journal of Experimental Child Psychology* 110 (2011): 213–26.

[55] E. Ritvo, J. Q. Delrosso, and C. LaRiche, C., "Psychosocial Judgments and Perceptions with Acne Vulgaris: A Blinded Controlled Comparison of Adult and Peer Evaluations," *Biosocial Medicine* 5, no. 1 (Aug. 26, 2011), doi10:1186/1`751-0759-5-11.

[56] F. de Zulueta, *From Pain to Violence: The Chaotic Roots of Destructiveness* (Hoboken: Publisher, 2006), 342.

[57] D. A. Friedman, *Jewish Pastoral Care: A Practical Handbook from Traditional & Contemporary Sources*, 2nd ed. (Woodstock: Jewish Lights Publishing: Public Affairs, 2010).

[58] L. M. Mayer and W. W. Blome, "The Importance of Early Targeted Intervention: The Effect of Family, Maternal and Child Characteristics on the Use of Physical Discipline," *Journal of Human Behavior and Social Environment* 23 (2013): 144–58, Doi:10.1080/109011359.2013.747406.

[59] L. Kaplan, "Spare the Rod and Spoil the Child," Temple Israel, Wilkes Barre, PA, Ohio: Center for Effective Discipline, 2013, www.stophitting.com/index.php/page=jewish.

[60] J. Telushkin, *Jewish Literacy* (New York: Random House, 2002), 192–93.

[61] W. Kolbrenner, *The Perils of the "Potch": Spare the Rod and Spoil the Child* (New York: Jewish Week, 2012).

[62] B. Nolan, ("St. Augustine Board Struggle Is Settled: Paddling Is Banned," *Times Picayune*, December 23, 2011.

[63] T. Johnson, "Paddle and Shield: Tom Johnson's Letter to the South Carolina Legislature," January 27, 2010,

[64] K. Joyce, *The Child Catchers* (New York: Public Affairs, 2013).

Chapter 4: Captain Kangaroo, Other Animals, and Corporal Punishment

[65] V. Schade, *Secrets of a Dog Trainer* (New York: Wiley)2014.

[66] T. Gellar, *The Loved Dog: The Nonaggressive Way to Teach Your Dog Good Behavior* (New York: Simon and Shuster, 2007).

[67] M. Cusac, *Cruel and Unusual Punishment: The Culture of Punishment in America* (New Haven: Yale).

[68] T. Hogg, *Secrets of the Baby Whisperer for Toddlers* (New York: Ballantine, 2013).

[69] C.B. Flynn, "Exploring the Link Between Corporal Punishment and Children's Cruelty to Animals," *Journal of Marriage and the Family* 61 (1999): 971–81.

[70] B. Keeshan, "Corporal Punishment," *Humanist* 39 (Nov. and Dec., 1988):10–12.

[71] L. Cozolino, *The Social Neuroscience of Education: Optimizing Learning and Attachment in the Classroom* (New York: Norton, 2013).

[72] J. Gottman and N. Jacobson, *When Men Batter Women* (New York: Simon and Schuster, 2011).

[73] J. Gottman and J. Declaire, *Raising an Emotionally Healthy Child: The Heart of Parenting* (New York: Fireside, 1997).

Chapter 5: My Story Isn't Unbeatable

[74] S. M. Fleischman, *The History of the Jewish Foster Home and Orphan Asylum of Philadelphia, 1855, New York, 1905* (New York: General Books, 2009).

[75] D. Gottlieb, in R. Chillott, "Do I Make You Uncomfortable?" *Psychology Today* 46, no. 6 (Dec. 2013), 77.

Chapter 6: Who is Bullying Whom?

[76] R. Pring, *Personal and Social Education in the Curriculum* (London: Hoddard and Stoughton, 1984), 33.

[77] K. Brohl, *Social Service Workplace Bullying: Betrayal of Good Intentions* (New York: Lyceum, 2013).

[78] S. Cleaver, *Why Are We Still Hitting?*(New York: Scholastic Press, 2013).

[79] S. Strean, *Psychoanalytical Approaches to the Hostile and Violent Client* (New York: Haworth, 1984).

[80] S. W. Twemlow, P. Fonagy, P. Sacco, and J. R. Brethour, "Teachers Who Bully Students: A Hidden Trauma," *International Journal of Social Psychiatry* 52 (2013): 187–98.

[81] J. Garberino and E. deLara, *Words Can Hurt Forever* (New York: Free Press, 2002), 26

[82] M. M. Alward, "Is Your Child's Teacher a Bully?" Local school-directory.com, 2006, http://www.a-better-child.org/page/933699.

[83] Twemlow et al.

[84] D.Hembree, "The Tragic Side of Classroom Punishment," *Hippocrates* (March/April 1988).

[85] L. Hyman, L. and P. Snook, *The Case Against Spanking: How to Discipline Your Child without Hitting* (New York: Wiley, 1997).

[86] C. Ross, South Suicidal National Center, Burlington, VT, 1989, http://healthvermont.gov/family/injury/suicide_prevent aspx.

[87] E. U. Shin, "The Happy School Campaign in Korea," *Brain World* 1, no. 2 (fall 2010): 48–49.

[88] G. Collins, *Everything Is Bigger in Texas: How the Lone Star State Hijacked the American Agenda* (New York: Norton, 2012).

[89] B. D. Perry and M. Szalavitz, *Born for Love: Why Empathy Is Essential and Endangered* (New York: Morrow, 2011).

[90] E. Gershoff, "More Harm Than Good: A Summary of the Research on the Intended and Unintended Effects of Corporal Punishment," *Law and Contemporary Problems* 73 (2010), no. 31: 31–56.

[91] H. Kempe, E. H. Keifer, and R. D. Krugman, *The Battered Child* (Chicago: University Press, 1997).

[92] Colorado Accommodation Model (2013–2014), *Building Bridges for the Future,* Colorado. www.cde.state.co/us/desped/building bribges

[93] M. Szalalavitz, "Why Autistic Kids Make Easy Targets for School Bullies, *Time* (2012)..

[94] Zhou, K., "Alarming! School Bullies Attack Almost Half of Kids with Autism," Takepart, September 12, 2012,

http://www.takepart.com/article/2012/09/04/school-bullies-attack-almost-half-kids-who-have-autism.

[95] T. D. George, *Untangling the Mind* (New York: Harper, 2013).

[96] A. L. Beane, "Bully-Free Classroom," Minnesota Department of Education, 2012, www.cde.state.co.us/cdesped/building bridges.

Chapter 7: Science Be Damned

[97] R. Peters-Bennett, "Spanking Is a Brain Bath," Feb. 1, 2013, http://www.topspanking.org./2013/02/01/spanking-is-a-brain-bath.

[98] S. Gerhardt, *The Selfish Society: How We Forgot to Love and Made Money Instead"* (London: Simon and Schuster, 2010), 131.

[99] Gerhardt, 29.

[100] *Brain World*, "Beliefs and Values That Changed Education Since 1965: Change in Beliefs and Values 1990–2010, United Nations International Education Association, 56–57.

[101] M. Seligman, Introduction in *Everyday Parenting Toolkit* (New York: Houghton Mifflin, 2013).

[102] A. Kazdin, *Everyday Parenting Toolkit* (New York: Houghton Mifflin, 2013).

[103] E. Gershoff, "More Harm Than Good: A Summary of the Research on the Intended and Unintended Effects of Corporal Punishment," *Law and Contemporary Problems* 73 (2010), no. 31: 31–56.

[104] Kazdin, 88–89.

[105] A. Bandura, *Social Foundation of Thought and Action: A Social Cognitive Theory* (New York: Prentice-Hall, 1985).

[106] T. B. Brazelton, *Learning to Listen: A Life Caring for Children* (New York: Perseus, 2013).

[107] D. Brent and M. Silverstein, "1777–1778: Shedding Light on the Long Shadow of Childhood Adversity." *JAMA* 17 (May 1, 2013): 861–62.

[108] G. Scott, *The History of Corporal Punishment* (London: TW Laurie Ltd., 1938), 10–1

[109] Ibid.

[110] R.J. Stoller, Perversion: the Erotic Form of Hatred (London:Karnak,1975),16.

[111] J. Friel and D. O. Freil, *The Power and Grace of Nasty and Nice* (Deerfield Beach, FL: HCL, 2012).

[112] A. M. Kaplan, H. I. Kaplan, and H. S. Freedman, *Comprehensive Textbook of Psychiatry* (New York: Williams and Wilkins, 1967).

[113] R. Brehl, "For the Health of Our Society: 'Normal' Child Abuse Prevention," Psychology Central, 2013, http://www.blogs.psychcentral.com/attachment/2013/04/for-the-health.

[114] R. McCall and C. Groark, "The Future of Applied Child Development, Research, and Social Policy," *Child Development* 71 (2000), no. 1:197–204.

[115] A. Becker-Weidman, A. Lehrman, and D. LeBow, *The Attachment Therapy Companion* (New York: Norton, 2012), 49–50.

[116] Domestic Violence Resource Center, "Hillsboro Colorado: Net Raising." Accessed. November 11 ,2014 www.dvrc-or.org

[117] N. Davis, S. Clark, M. Davis, and G. Freed, "Father's Depression Related to Positive and Negative Parenting Behaviors with 1 Year Old Children. *Pediatrics* (March 14, 2011).

[118] V. J. Felitti et al., "Relationship of Childhood Abuse and Household Dysfunction to Many Leading Causes of Death in Adults: The Adverse Experience (ACE) Study," *American Journal of Preventive Medicine* 14, no. 4 (May 1988):245–58.

[119] R. J. Marzano, J. S. Marzano, and D. J. Pickering, *Classroom Management That Works: Research Based Strategies for Every Teacher* (Alexandria, VA: Association for Supervision and Curriculum Development, 2003).

[120] R.A.Thompson and J. Wyatt.. Current Research on Child Maltreatment: Implications for Education. Educational Psychology Review. 11, no.3,1999.

[121] *National Health and National Safety Performance Standards: Guidelines for Out of Home Child Care Placements* (Washington, DC: American

Public Health Association, National Center for Education in Maternal and Child Health, 1992).

[122] A. Bandura, 1985.

[123] B. D. Perry, .

[124] M. Iacobonni, *Mirroring People: The Science of Empathy and How We Connect with Others* (New York: Farrar, 2009).

[125] D. D. Simons and S. K. Wurtele, "Relations between Parents' Use of Corporal Punishment and Their Endorsement of Spanking and Hitting," *Child Abuse and Neglect* 34 (2010): 639–46.

[126] C. Phrend, "Child-Abuse Injuries on the Rise, 2012, http://abc-news.go.com/Health/Wellness/child   -abuse-injuries-rise/story/id=17364578.

[127] J. Crandall and F. Vida, "Support for Spanking: Most Americans Think Corporal Punishment is O.K.," Accessed October 13, 2013, abcnews.com/sections/us/DailyNews/spanking...poll021108html.

Chapter 8: Sports and Wrestling with "Corporal Punishment"

[128] O. Katrandjanian, "'If Fred Got Two Beatings a Day' Homework Asks," ABC News, 2012, www.wcti12.com/Homework-Asks-If- Fred-Got-Two-Beatings.

[129] B. deLench, *Home Team Advantage: Critical Role of Moms in Team Sports* (New York: Harper Collins, 2006).

[130] L. Zinser, "A Sad History of Abusive Coaches," *New York Times*, April 13, 2013.

[131] S. Paolantonio, *How Football Changes America* (Chicago: Triumph, 2008).

[132] B. deLench).

[133] H. Storm, *Go Girl: Raising Happy, Healthy, Confident, and Successful Girls through Sports* (Naperville, IL: Sourcebooks, 2002), 99.

[134] J. West, *West by West: My Charmed Tormented Life* (New York: Little Brown, 2011).

Chapter 9: History of Child Maltreatment

[135] M. Mead and R. Metra, *Study Culture at a Distance* (Chicago: Berghahn, 2000).

[136] E. Young-Bruehl, *Childism* (New Haven: Yale University Press, 2013).

[137] K. B. Walant, *Creating the Capacity for Attachment: Treating Addictions and the Alienated Self,* (London: Aronson, 1995), 71.

[138] Paine, T., quoted in J. Lewis, "Inspiration and Wisdom in the Writings of Thomas Paine, Accessed January 7, 2013, www.positive-atheism.org/hist/lewtp005.htm.

[139] M.A.. Cusac, *Cruel and Unusual: The Culture of Punishment in America* (New Haven: Yale Press, 2009).

140 Samuel Gilgal, "Founding Father Benjamin Rush Speaks His Mind," Word Press.com, October 6, 2009, samuelatgilgal. wordpress/2009/founding-father.

141 M. Petit, *Presidents Helping Children*, (Washington, DC: Every Child Matters Education Fund, 2012).

142 A. Maurer and J. S. Wallerstein, *The Bible and the Rod: Alternatives to Corporal Punishment.*, vol. 1. (Berkeley: Generation Books, 1984).

143 G. Carter, "Advocacy Groups Link Paddling to Slavery," University of Alabama *Exponent Student Newspaper,* June 8, 2004, www.nospank.net/exponent.htm.

144 S. Coontz, *The Way We Never Were* (New York: Basic, 1993), 35.

145 H. Deutsch, *The Psychology of Women* (New York: Grune and Stratton, 1944).

146 A. Guttman, *A Democratic Education,* (Princeton: Princeton Press, 1987).

147 R. Yehuda, *Psychobiology of Posttraumatic Stress Disorder* (New York: NYU, 1980).

148 R. Dreikurs and V. Stolz, *Children, the Challenge* (New York: Penguin, 1990).

149 N. H. Azrin and R. N. Fox, *Toilet Training in Less than a Day* (New York: Pocket, 1986).

[150] Fraiberg, *The Magic Years: Understanding and Handling the Problems of Early Childhood* (New York: Fireside, 1996).

[151] R. Barkeley, *Your Defiant Child* (New York: Guilford, 2013).

[152] F. Cline and J. Fay, *Parenting with Love and Logic* (Colorado Springs: Nav Press, 2006).

[153] W. Cosby and A. Poussaint, *Come on, People* (New York: Thomas Nelson, 2007).

[154] J. Comer, *Leave No Child Behind: Preparing Today's Children for Tomorrow's World* (New York: Children's Defense Fund, 2004.

Chapter 10: Conclusion

[155] J. Fallon, *The Psychopath Inside: A Neuroscientist's Journey into the Dark Side of the Brain* (New York: Penguin, 2013).

[156] M. F. Roizen and M. Oz, M, *You Raising Your Child: The Owner's Manual from First Breath to First Grade* (New York: Free Press, 2010).

85634275R00098

Made in the USA
San Bernardino, CA
21 August 2018